Walt
Wo
Orlando

120th anniversary

Berlitz

- A 👉 in the text denotes a highly recommended sight
- A complete A–Z of practical information starts on p.103
- Extensive mapping on cover flaps and throughout text

Berlitz Publishing Company, Inc.

Princeton   Mexico City   Dublin   Eschborn   Singapore

Text:	Martin Gostelow
Editor:	Sarah Hudson
Photography:	Martin Gostelow, Jacques Bétant; © Universal Stu-dios Florida; © Busch Gardens, Tampa; Orlando/Or-ange County Convention and Visitors Bureau Inc.; © Wet 'n' Wild
Layout:	Media Content Marketing, Inc.
Cartography:	Geosystems

Disclaimer
The author, researchers and publishers of this guide specifically declare that
they are totally independent of the Walt Disney World Resort and of any and
all other members of the Disney corporate family. The material described in
this guide has not been approved in any manner by the Disney organization.
Within this guide, no attempt has been made by the author or publisher to in-
fringe copyrights or trademarks of the Walt Disney Company Inc. such as
Audio-Animatronics, EPCOT and *Captain EO*, which have been presented
only in those contexts to which they legally and properly belong, nor those
trademarks and copyrights pending.

*Found an error we should know about? Our editor would be happy
to hear from you, and a postcard would do. Although we make every
effort to ensure the accuracy of all the information in this book,
changes do occur.*

ISBN 2-8315-6298-8
Revised 1998 – First Printing April 1998

Printed in Switzerland by Weber SA, Bienne
019/804 REV

CONTENTS

Walt Disney World & Orlando

ORLANDO AND THE
THEME PARKS

Quite simply, Walt Disney World Resort, near Orlando in central Florida, is the biggest holiday attraction on earth. The Disney property covers an area of 113 sq km (44 sq miles) or 11,200 hectares (28,000 acres), almost the size of San Francisco. Orlando isn't Walt Disney World, however, and Walt Disney World isn't Orlando. For one thing, the resort is situated some 40 km (25 miles) southwest of the city, and much nearer the once-sleepy cattle town of Kissimmee. Mickey Mouse and his friends certainly triggered the boom, but lots of other attractions have clustered round as well, to benefit from the huge flow of visitors. The world's biggest supply of hotel beds in a single place, 130,000 at the last count, is ready and waiting to accommodate them.

Many visitors fly directly into Orlando International Airport, whose traffic has multiplied by a factor of 20 in the years since the advent of Disney. Others arrive in Miami, 353 km (220 miles) away to the south, with good roads and frequent flights from there to Orlando. In addition, huge numbers drive from all over North America — just check the licence plates of the cars in one of the parks and count the number of states represented. Train and bus services also link Orlando with the rest of Florida and with main U.S. cities.

Walt Disney World opened its gates to the public for the first time on Friday, 1 October, 1971, which was deliberately chosen as the quietest day in Florida's least busy month for tourism. Ready to learn from experience, the park's executives wished to avoid the traffic snarls and capacity crowds that had jammed California's Disneyland on its first day. Even so, 10,000 visitors came. By the day after Thanksgiving in late November 1971 the figure had risen to 60,000 and the park

All your favourite cartoon characters come alive in the theme parks.

was full. Since then, Walt Disney World has grown in popularity each year.

Walt Disney himself had prophesied that the park would never be finished, but he wasn't predicting slow progress: he meant that it would evolve and expand, and so it has proved. First there was the Magic Kingdom, a more ambitious version of Disneyland in California; then came the EPCOT Center, even bigger; and finally in 1989 the Disney-MGM Studios Theme Park added to the empire. All have grown since they opened, and a fourth theme park, the Animal Kingdom, opened its grounds to visitors in mid-1998. Initially there were three Disney hotels, now there are 14, offering up to 2,200 rooms each. Their designers are rewriting the book of resort architecture — they just don't know where to stop!

Walt Disney World is much more than an amusement park, or parks, and it's not just for children either. You might be surprised to learn that it's one of the most popular honeymoon destinations in the United States. In fact, the majority of its visitors are adults — for them Walt Disney World provides nightspots and bars in hotels as well as discos and clubs on Pleasure Island. With pools and sandy beaches (yes, this far from the sea), lakes and sailing, tennis courts, and more golf facilities than any Florida *golf* resort, you might stay within the Disney "borders" for your whole trip. Only, then you'd miss all the other attractions of the Orlando area.

Universal Studios Florida opened in 1990, but plans for studios here had been around for several years, ever since Orlando had gained its reputation as "Hollywood East." (Long enough in fact for Disney to get ahead and open Disney-MGM Studios first.) The idea of coming to central Florida was not simply to tap into the theme-park market, but also to take advantage of the climate and to reduce labour and other costs. A 178-hectare (444-acre) site was selected north of International Drive, close to the key I-4 interstate highway. The open spaces offered the chance to build rides and attractions as well as the real production facilities on a huge scale. Sets were made as accessible to visitors as possible, so that they would become part of the show. Investment in Universal Studios by the joint owners, MCA and the Rank Organization, reached around $630 million, and when you see the size of the

Songs and somersaults from the popular Blues Brothers are recreated regularly in the street at Universal studios.

operation and some of the technology, you'll understand where all the money went.

Sea World began in Florida in 1973 as an up-to-date version of the marine parks that have been a Florida tradition ever since the 1920s. Now it has grown and developed into much more than leaping dolphins, clowning sea lions, and parading penguins. Busch Entertainment Corporation, part of the giant brewing empire Anheuser-Busch, bought Sea World in 1989, adding it to their already existing properties — Busch Gardens in Tampa, and Cypress Gardens south of Orlando — and throwing down a challenge to Disney supremacy. They have multiplied the attractions and added to the variety, to make a visit to Sea World a logical part of any trip to Orlando.

Lookalikes turn up just about anywhere in the film studio theme parks.

After you've spent a few days in the theme parks, seen the impressively gaudy strip called International Drive, and driven up and down the I-4 and Highway 192 a few times, you may still wonder whether Orlando *does* have a city centre. The answer is yes, although millions who go straight from the airport to Walt Disney World or Kissimmee never see it. From the top of Disney's highest building, it's just a speck on the horizon. Even International Drive, halfway between, is 15 km (9 miles) from downtown Orlando.

Until the 1960s, Orlando was an old-fashioned inland town in a flat landscape dotted with lakes and swamps. True, it had several charming suburbs built by prosperous migrants who were retreating from northern winters, and it still has them, but all else has changed beyond recognition. First the space programme, based at nearby Cape Canaveral, attracted high-technology industries to the

Vintage impersonators bring motion picture history to life.

region. Then came the tourist boom, calling for huge numbers of people to work in the labour-intensive service sector. Those needed services, too, and so began the chain reaction.

There's been a population explosion, and compared with much of Florida, it's a younger crowd. Many big companies moved their headquarters here, and sports stars have made it their home, making Orlando the hub of central Florida, with mushrooming steel-and-glass towers and headlong development. Unsurprisingly, the presence of big business didn't lure many people away from the theme parks, so Orlando decided to inject some fun with an entertainment complex of its own, restoring several old buildings to create the food and entertainment complex of Church Street Station.

Excellent roads put all the attractions nearby within easy reach. Less than an hour's drive east is the Atlantic Coast and Kennedy Space Center, with the Gulf Coast not much farther away to the west. There's enough to occupy several holidays. No wonder people keep returning.

THE WALT DISNEY STORY

Walter Elias Disney was born on 5 December, 1901, in Chicago. His father was a building contractor of Anglo-Irish stock and Canadian birth. When Walt was still a toddler, the family moved to a farm in Marcelina, Missouri. All the children, even the youngest, had to help on the farm, but Walt showed an interest in drawing from an early age and took his first art lessons in Kansas City when he was 14. In 1919 he served as an ambulance driver with the U.S. Army in France, too late to witness action in World War I. As surviving photographs show, he still drew during this period, though his talents were confined to caricatures on his ambulance and fake medals on his buddies' jackets.

He had seen the simple animated films of the time, and was sure he could do better. In Kansas City he teamed up with artist Ubbe "Ub" Iwerks to make commercials and animated versions of Cinderella and Robin Hood. He formed a partnership with his older brother Roy to produce a series of shorts called *Alice in Cartoonland*, combining live action and animation (a formula Disney was to return to years later with *Mary Poppins*).

Disney Goes to Hollywood

The *Alice* series enjoyed some success, but the costs broke the new studio. Disney packed his bags and moved to Los Angeles in 1923, determined to make animated films that were more than crude fillers. He wanted to create characters who had a life of their own and emotions that people could recognize. Iwerks joined him to look after the artwork and Roy Disney, who was already in California, ran the business side.

The pattern was soon set. Disney had the ideas and, as he explained, "pollinated" the various departments, like a bee moving from flower to flower. By 1926 he had stopped drawing and he was sometimes embarrassed later when children assumed he had created his films singlehanded — and yet he couldn't do them a sketch of Pluto or Goofy. *Oswald the Lucky Rabbit* brought recognition, but Disney lost the rights to the character in a contractual dispute with a New York distributor. He learned his lesson: from then on he retained absolute control of his company's creations and defended them fiercely with copyrights and trademarks.

Everyone wants an autograph from a Disney star.

According to Disney, he was on a train back from New York when he came up with the idea of a new hero, a mouse to be called... Mortimer! When he told his wife, Lillian, she wisely suggested Mickey instead. Ub Iwerks drew the soon-to-be-famous character to Walt's satisfaction, with the famous circular ears, velvet trousers, big round-toed shoes, and four-finger gloves.

It was 1927, and Mickey Mouse appeared in the silent film *Plane Crazy*, which came out at the same time as the first-ever talking picture, *The Jazz Singer*. Sensing the way the wind was blowing, Disney quickly withdrew his film, and re-released it with a soundtrack. In 1928, Mickey starred in the first animated film with sound, *Steamboat Willie*. Walt himself was the provider of Mickey's falsetto voice (and continued in that role for many years). Minnie Mouse made her debut in the same film, when Mickey hauled her on board with a boathook.

Steamboat Willie and its stars were a huge success. In some countries the characters were given new names (in Italy Mickey was called Topolino, and it was no coincidence when the very same name was given to Fiat's popular car).

Disney's dream had come true. The sheer quality of the work, the attention to detail, the wit and talent of the artists and his own perfectionism had lifted animated films to new heights. He had the respect of film-makers, who watched Disney productions for new ideas. The public loved the characters. In 1934, Donald Duck's arrival brought a personality to counteract Mickey's essential cheerfulness. The malicious, irascible bird in the silly sailor suit whose pride always led to a fall became an even bigger favourite than Mickey.

Disney was a pioneer in the use of colour, with *Flowers and Trees,* in 1933, and in some of the *Silly Symphony* series in the mid-1930s. A taste of things to come, these stories were set in the kinds of fairy-tale landscape that sprang to life in the theme parks many years later.

Young thrill-seekers brace themselves for the next disaster, as they take a ride through Catastrophe Canyon.

Walt Disney was now ready to climb the ultimate mountain, even if the studio's accountants were alarmed at the cost. He was planning the first full-length animated feature film, *Snow White and the Seven Dwarfs*. It's hard now to imagine how daring a proposal this seemed — and was. To attain the quality he had in mind, very fine artwork was needed. In addition, an 83-minute film didn't use just ten times the drawings and painted "cels" (see page 23) as an 8-minute film. Far *more* than that were needed to give the human characters the smooth movements of live actors. He hired 300 new artists (bringing the total to 750); the job still took over two years.

Finally, in late 1937, *Snow White and the Seven Dwarfs* was given a star-studded première in Hollywood, the first ever for an animated production. That first audience was enchanted, and dissolved into laughter and tears as millions have done since. The film was a hit and won a special Academy Award: a big Oscar for Snow White and seven little ones for the dwarfs. *Pinocchio,* an even more intricate achievement, followed in 1940.

Disney broke new ground again in 1940 with *Fantasia*, setting beautiful, funny, and bizarre scenes to the music of Bach, Beethoven, Tchaikovsky, and Stravinsky. Mickey Mouse played *The Sorcerer's Apprentice*, whose delusions of omnipotence unleash forces beyond his control. It was almost a metaphor for the war that had begun in Europe and was about to enmesh the United States. When it did, Disney Studios made training films, with GIs adopting the suitably aggressive Donald Duck in commando uniform as a mascot.

Building the Dream

After World War II, Disney made *Song of the South*, combining live action and animation. This was followed by a number of all-live films including *Treasure Island, Swiss Family Robin-*

son, and *20,000 Leagues Under the Sea,* which generated ideas for the future theme parks. The animated features of the 1950s — *Cinderella, Alice in Wonderland, Peter Pan* and *Sleeping Beauty* — also served as inspiration for the theme parks.

Disney had always loved the idea of amusement parks, but when he would visit some with his daughters, they seemed tawdry and run-down. Worse still, they were unimaginative. Some operators were simply in it for a fast buck, others were downright dishonest. Since the 1930s, Disney had thought of creating his own version.

By 1947, on doctors' orders, Disney was supposed to be relaxing a bit, but for him that just meant throwing himself into a new project, this time a model railway which got bigger and bigger, until he had no more room for it... unless he built a theme park, of course; then he'd have all the space he needed. He presented the plan to his more cautious brother Roy, who wouldn't agree to invest more than $10,000 in the "screwy idea." As Walt Disney's story goes, he raised the capital himself, on his life insurance policy.

By 1952 he had set up a company, WED (his initials) and sketched out the plans. He acquired 65 hectares (160 acres) of land in Anaheim, on the southern edge of Los Angeles. Now he could build not only a railway, but a complete "Disneyland," and people it with his characters. His designers created a huge stage set, on which visitors moved from scene to scene like stars of the show. It was more than a fairground or an amusement park. There had never been anything like it.

Disneyland opened on 17 July, 1955, an overwhelming success, with more than 4 million visitors in the first year, rising to 10 million a year as its fame spread. The number of attractions doubled, while executives learned from experience how to handle such unprecedented numbers. But Disney was not entirely happy. Fast-food and souvenir shops had spread to the borders of Disneyland, creaming off revenues he felt should belong to Walt Disney Productions.

A New World in Florida

Disney was determined not to make the same mistake twice. As he began searching for a suitable theme park site in the eastern United States, one prerequisite was a great

View from above: Orlando seen from a hot air balloon.

deal of real estate. The others were a year-round sunny climate and good travel connections that could expand to handle the traffic. The scouts found what he was looking for in central Florida, near the quiet town of Orlando. Nominees started to buy land, eventually picking up 11,000 hectares (27,500 acres) by 1964 at the reasonable cost of $6 million. If word had got out that Disney was behind it, prices would have rocketed. (When it did, they did, multiplying a hundredfold overnight).

Disney planned a park on the lines of Disneyland, except larger, but his dream went far beyond. He envisaged nothing less than a "living, breathing city of the future," his "Experimental Prototype Community of Tomorrow," or EPCOT. He outlined his plan in a film, but sadly, it was the last he was to make. In December 1966, he died quite suddenly, of complications following surgery for lung cancer.

Roy O. Disney had not always seen eye-to-eye with his brother, but they had recently set aside their differences, and

Roy became chairman of Walt Disney Productions. At his suggestion, the Florida project was given the name Walt Disney World — a generous tribute to his brother. ("Resort" was added to emphasize the range of activities.)

Preparation began in 1967 and construction followed in 1969. By October 1971, the Magic Kingdom was open. This time, guests could stay in Disney hotels, swim, play golf and tennis, dine, and be entertained without leaving Disney territory. When everyone from top executives to the newest cast member had to help park cars or cook hot-dogs, it began a tradition — cross-utilization, or "X-U" in Disney parlance.

EPCOT took longer to realize. It was hard to reconcile a harmonious "living community" with streams of visitors in their millions, but the Disney organization had gained a lot of experience at various World Fairs, and the EPCOT Center, opened in 1982, does resemble a twin-centre World's Fair. Future World recalls the celebration of technology Disney had proposed, while World Showcase, comprising the pavilions of several nations, is quite different. But both are true to Walt's dictum: "I would rather entertain and hope that people learn, than educate and hope they're entertained."

Tokyo Disneyland followed in 1983 and was another hit. Soon the parks became

Experience a bit of Chinese culture at the EPCOT Center.

financially more important than film-making. Believing that EPCOT's costs and the shortage of new film successes had weakened Walt Disney Productions, outside interests planned a take-over. Perhaps it was just lucky, but the 50th birthday of gutsy little Donald Duck in 1984 coincided with the company's survival and a new era.

Back on Top

As the dust settled, Michael Eisner became the chairman and chief executive. The Disney family connection continued when Roy E. Disney, son of Roy O., became head of animation. The Disney organization was transformed with a string of film successes, new television series, and fresh licensing contracts for Disney products. One of Eisner's first acts was to sign an agreement with the French for the building of the Euro Disney Resort east of Paris. It opened in April 1992.

The attractions of Walt Disney World were increased with the 1989 openings of Typhoon Lagoon and Pleasure Island, and a *third* theme park celebrating the company's re-dedication to its roots in the movie business. Disney-MGM Studios has real film sets and TV studios where actual productions take shape, as well as an animation department, which created long sequences for *Beauty and the Beast* and *Aladdin*, full-length features in the tradition of Walt Disney's best.

Never content to rest on its laurels, Disney continues to develop its staggering collection of resorts, exhibits, and parks. Most notably, Disney has created a fourth major theme park, the Animal Kingdom. Described as a "live-animal adventure park," this 202-hectare (500-acre) site opened in mid-1998 with fantastic rides, herds of wild animals, and exotic landscapes where one might glimpse those zoological rarities, unicorns and dragons.

WHERE TO GO

THE WALT DISNEY WORLD RESORT

The Walt Disney World Resort now contains four immense theme parks and several other major attractions which could almost rank as theme parks in their own right. Naturally, there's also plenty to do and see beyond Disney borders. Faced with so many possibilities, you will need a plan of action, especially if this is your first visit or your time is limited. How do you decide what to do, and the order in which to do it? We don't suggest a rigid schedule, but unless you allocate your time wisely, you'll find it difficult to take full advantage of all that's on offer.

Your first step is to abandon any idea of "seeing everything." With the help of this guide, choose which parks you want to visit and then the rides and attractions that most appeal to you. On pages 103-127 you will find general information on transport, first aid, lost property, etc., but to begin with here are some hints on how to tackle Walt Disney World.

A Few Pointers

Peak times are Christmas and early January, the weeks before and at Easter, mid-June to late August, and long weekend holidays in the United States, such as Thanksgiving in late November. Winter in central Florida is generally delightful, and it's hot and humid in the summer, but you can cool off in hotel pools and waterparks and enjoy spending more time outside in the evenings. There is really no bad time to visit.

You can buy one-day, one-park tickets, although such a short visit isn't recommended. If you do have only one day, however, select one park and enjoy it as an appetizer. For longer visits, Walt Disney World sells money-saving passes for four days (all theme parks) and five days (all theme parks as well as other attractions), and an added incentive is that passes don't have to be used on consecutive days.

Which park should you visit first? The **Magic Kingdom** (see page 22) is what first comes to mind when most people think of Walt Disney World. Stroll down spick-and-span Main Street, USA to reach the six other "lands": Adventureland, Frontierland, Liberty Square, Fantasyland, Mickey's Toontown Fair, and Tomorrowland. The Magic Kingdom is where you are most likely to meet any Disney characters, though they do also appear in other parks.

Film fans will naturally be drawn to **Disney-MGM Studios** (see page 49). It was Disney productions that inspired *Beauty and the Beast* and *The Voyage of the Little Mermaid*, but not all the attractions have Disney origins. You'll see stunts from the Indiana Jones films and ride in the Star Tours flight simulator on a giddy trip inspired by George Lucas's film *Star Wars*. Backstage, you can see both film and television production in progress, and look over the shoulders of artists working on new animated feature films.

The **EPCOT Center** (see page 37) will appeal more to (and is aimed at) older children and adults. EPCOT set out to be more serious than its magical neighbour, but they couldn't resist the temptation to add a lot more fun — and who's complaining? The huge park comprises two areas, Future World and World Showcase. The first highlights the worlds of energy, health,

Disney street signs help direct your imagination.

travel, communications, the land, the seas, and the imagination, while World Showcase presents the culture, products, and cuisines of 11 countries. Brilliant replicas of famous buildings and scaled-down examples of regional architecture are home to rides, 360° Circle-Vision films, and restaurants.

The newest theme park, opened in late April 1998, is **Disney's Animal Kingdom**, featuring dinosaurs and the wilds of Africa.

The Magic Kingdom

If you're staying at one of the resorts on the monorail system, that is the quickest way to reach the attractions. If your Disney accommodation is not on the monorail, you can take one of the free Walt Disney World buses. If you drive yourself, you'll be directed to the vast car park. Guests at a Dis-

---

Making the Most of Your Time: an Eight-Point Plan

1. Make a choice of rides and attractions for each park. Look at the (free) park maps to work out a route.
2. It will save time if you buy tickets (or four- or five-day passes) in advance at Walt Disney World hotels or travel agents.
3. If you can, arrive early at the entrance, before the gates open (see page 26). That way, you'll use your ticket to the full.
4. Look at the Entertainment Schedule leaflet to check the times of parades and special events.
5. Have lunch early, or late, to avoid the midday rush.
6. Leave any shopping until after the rides.
7. Visit indoor and sit-down shows in the early afternoon — you'll appreciate the shade and air-conditioning.
8. Leave time for relaxation, especially if you have small children. You may want to take a siesta at your hotel (remember to get your hand stamped to allow you to re-enter).

ney property have free parking if they show their hotel ID card. Note where you leave your car — rows are numbered but the spaces are not, and areas are named. If you think there's a danger you'll forget whether you're in Grumpy, Sleepy, or Dopey, write down the details! To get to the park from the car park you can choose between a 600-passenger two-decker ferryboat or a smooth monorail train: either way will take no more than a few minutes.

At the **Transportation and Ticket Center** (TTC) you can buy a one-day ticket for the Magic Kingdom or a four- or five-day multi-park pass.

Main Street, USA

Beyond the tracks and station of the Walt Disney World Railroad, the scene opens out into **Town Square**, an idealized version of a small American town centre from the year 1900. It buzzes with action the whole day, with bands playing and Disney characters greeting guests and signing autographs.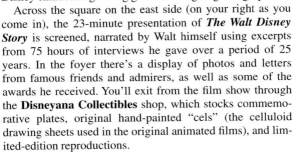

Across the square on the east side (on your right as you come in), the 23-minute presentation of *The Walt Disney Story* is screened, narrated by Walt himself using excerpts from 75 hours of interviews he gave over a period of 25 years. In the foyer there's a display of photos and letters from famous friends and admirers, as well as some of the awards he received. You'll exit from the film show through the **Disneyana Collectibles** shop, which stocks commemorative plates, original hand-painted "cels" (the celluloid drawing sheets used in the original animated films), and limited-edition reproductions.

You can board a horsedrawn trolley, horseless carriage, omnibus to **Cinderella Castle** (see page 31), or fire engine to ride down Main Street, or you might prefer to stroll along, checking out the shops and a couple of attractions from by-

MAGIC KINGDOM

N

Lake Mable

South Lake

Osprey Ridge Golf Course

Bonnet Creek Golf Club

Eagle Pines Golf Course

.75 mi

.5

.25

0

VISTA

RI

Bay Lake

BIG PINE DRIVE

RIVER COUNTRY

FORT WILDERNESS

DISCOVERY ISLAND

TRAIL

FRONTIER WAY

DISNEY'S FORT WILDERNESS RESORT AND CAMPGROUND

REAMS RD

Security Booth

Mickey's Toontown Fair

Cinderella Castle

Tomorrowland

Disney's Contemporary Resort

Disney's Wilderness Lodge

Ticket and Transportation Center

VISTA BL

Fantasyland

MAGIC KINGDOM

Liberty Square

Main Street U.S.A.

Monorail

Magic Kingdom Main Entrance/

Frontierland

Adventureland

Seven Seas Lagoon

Disney's Fairy Tale Wedding Pavilion

Disney's Polynesian Resort

SEVEN SEAS DR

MAGIC KINGDOM PARKING

Walt Disney World Speedway

WAY

Disney's Grand Floridian Beach Resort

FLORIDIAN

Shades of Green

Palm Golf Course

ISLAND ROAD

Magnolia Golf Course

gone days. On the right, the **Main Street Cinema** presents continuous comic classics, including the historic *Steamboat Willie* (see page 13), the film that was Mickey Mouse's first hit and which also marked Minnie Mouse's debut. Although it did have a soundtrack, it is silent here because six films are shown at once, on screens all round the room. For this same reason, you have to stand.

A Main Street trolley takes you back to the turn of the

Across the street and down the little alley, you can get an old-fashioned shave or a haircut at **Harmony Barber Shop**. As often as not, a barbershop quartet is on hand to keep you entertained with romantic melodies. **Main Street Book Store** has the biggest collection of cards, books on the cinema, and a host of children's books based on Disney films. Close by, you'll see — not to mention hear — **Penny Arcade**. Technology ranging over the last hundred years provides fun for, yes, a penny (one cent), a nickel, dime, or quarter. You won't *win* any money, though. In this eclectic tribute to coin-op entertainment, hand-crank movies vie for attention alongside state-of-the-art video games. Memories will recall some of the pinball games.

The circular **Plaza**, ringed by water, is the heart of the Magic Kingdom, with bridges and walkways to its different lands leading off like spokes of a wheel. On busy days, even if you've missed rope-drop (see page 26), you could still try to beat the rush by heading for the most popular rides first: Space Mountain in Tomorrowland (see page 37), or Big Thunder and Splash Mountain in Frontierland (page 28). Tiny children might do well to escort parents to Dumbo the Flying Elephant (see page 31).

You may have formulated a plan for your journey. Here we have chosen to go clockwise, starting with a sharp left turn at the Plaza to Adventureland.

Adventureland

The **Swiss Family Treehouse**, doubtless the biggest treehouse you've ever seen, is built in amongst the branches of a banyan that's almost a one-tree forest. Wood would have been too much of a fire risk, so it's made of concrete and the leaves are synthetic. You climb up winding stairways through the home of

---

On Your Marks...

If you've ever seen the start of the London or Boston marathons, you'll have an idea of what "rope-drop" is like, except that many of those runners are all dressed the same, whereas the Magic Kingdom's early birds are the most variegated, colourful crowd imaginable.

At the end of Main Street they assemble during the hour between main gate opening and the official opening, held back from their goals by a simple rope across the road. Nobody pushes. What is it about Walt Disney World that makes everyone so well-behaved?

At 9am sharp, the two cast members in charge open a gap in the middle and move the rope aside. (They used to drop it, but there was a risk of people tripping.) A wedge of assorted humanity, led by the most agile, heads through like a flying arrow, before splitting into left, centre, and right-hand streams. The leftists are making for Frontierland. The centre party goes for the passage through Cinderella Castle on the way to the attractions of Fantasyland, and the charge of the right brigade is bound for Space Mountain.

---

the famous shipwrecked Robinson family, seeing how they lived after the disaster. (The classic novel *The Swiss Family Robinson* was the subject of a live-action Disney film.)

In **Jungle Cruise**, the vegetation is real enough and some of it needs tender loving care to keep it warm and moist, even with the Florida summer. The mechanical lions roar and the giraffes, hippos, and bathing elephants look pretty convincing.

Geography goes haywire as you travel through the African plains and glimpse a Cambodian temple, while the captain keeps up a continuous jokey commentary. Across the way, in **Tropical Serenade**, the Enchanted Tiki Birds, housed under a Balinese-looking pagoda, are some of the earliest products of Disney's Audio-Animatronics technology.

Perennially popular, the **Pirates of the Caribbean** get up to all kinds of skullduggery in a raid on an island fort, from the opening bombardment to a most drunken climax. Your ship sails through it all as the battle rages, and smaller children could well be frightened by some of the (quite realistic) scenes of pillage, slaughter, and mayhem. The way the buccaneers treat their women captives is hardly correct, either.

Your adventures have just begun. A short stroll takes you to the front of Cinderella Castle, from where you can follow the way left along a little street of shops and snack bars, and turn left again. There is also a useful short-cut, down the little alley right opposite the Swiss Family Treehouse. Either way, you'll arrive in the Wild West.

Frontierland

The frontier is of course that of the American Wild West during the 19th century, when pioneers panned for gold or drove their cattle across the range. The cast dresses for the part, in kerchiefs and denim, bonnets and gingham, while the architecture runs the full gamut from log cabin to fancy façade. Even the vegetation is vetted for authenticity.

Performed several times a day, the **Diamond Horseshoe Saloon Revue and Medicine Show** always seems to have a full house. Its 30 minutes of song, dance, and comedy are certainly delivered with unflagging verve by a terrific cast. Seating is on a first-come, first-serve basis, with shows running continuously throughout the day.

At the explosive **Frontierland Shootin' Arcade** there are neither bullets nor pellets, but infra-red beams fired by converted hunting rifles. Otherwise, you might be in Tombstone, Arizona, in Wyatt Earp's day. Hits trigger off hilarious effects and the sound system provides appropriate screaming ricochets and howlin' coyotes. To stop you from hogging the action, there's a 50-cent charge for each round of 25 shots.

Along the same side of the street, in **Country Bear Jamboree** (or Vacation Hoedown), Audio-Animatronic characters perform a hilarious 15-minute stage show for country music fans.

Two of the highest hills in Florida are to be found here in the Magic Kingdom, where once there was only the flattest swamp. On **Splash Mountain** your boat slowly and inexorably climbs the watery slopes, winding up your anticipation. Scenes along the way come from *Song of the South*, the part-live, part-animated movie with Brer Rabbit and Brer Fox. You pass through tunnels, twists, and turns before emerging over five storeys up, where you'll hang in space before racing headlong down the 45-degree slope (which feels like a vertical drop) into the briar-fringed pool below. You'll definitely get wet, so cover your cameras, and vertigo sufferers abstain! Take note of the string of boarding restrictions — for example, nobody who suffers from back or neck problems should take the ride.

The same restrictions apply on **Big Thunder Mountain Railroad**, although it's funny rather than frightening. There are no falls as precipitate as those on Splash Mountain and certainly nothing as violent as on Space Mountain (see page 37).

Genuine mining equipment from days gone by litters the hillside and (not so genuine) dinosaur bones stick out from the slopes where you climb on board a "runaway" mine train that chugs to the top of the hill before rushing down at breakneck speed round unlikely bends before regaining the safety of the station.

You reach **Tom Sawyer Island** by raft. In complete contrast to the rest of the Magic Kingdom, more adventurous children can run around here on their own, firing the guns of Fort Sam Clemens, crossing swaying bridges, and exploring the caves and interesting secret passages. This can be a time-consuming expedition, though, and is perhaps best kept for a second visit. Note that Tom Sawyer Island closes at dusk.

Liberty Square

Just across the way from the wooden shacks of the Wild West, you'll have spotted a more elegant building of the Colonial era. The **Hall of Presidents** brings to life *every* American president from George Washington onwards. Each of them takes a bow on stage as they're introduced by the voice of poet Maya Angelou. First there's a five-screen, upbeat history of the U.S. Constitution (with

The "rope drop" — the start of an exciting day at Disney begins at 9am sharp.

the best seats at the back). Schedule the 25-minute show for a time when you feel like sitting down out of the sun.

You'll be tempted to try both of the two types of vessels that ply the **Rivers of America**, but it's sensible to choose just one — whichever of them has a shorter delay. As a rule, that will be the *Liberty Square Stern Wheeler*, recalling the heyday of the stylish paddle steamer. The alternative trip is on one of the **Mike Fink Keelboats**, named after an early American captain. Both take you past much the same forest scenery, animals, and occasional events on the river banks in a delightful and gentle experience.

As a contrast, you could give yourself a real fright in the **Haunted Mansion,** where, count them if you can, 999 ghosts emerge from the dark grinning and jumping. It's all very good-humoured, but still not for the very small or very nervous. You'll have time to try to puzzle out how some of the special effects ac-

---

Parades

Daily in the **Magic Kingdom,** the carnival-style afternoon parade (usually at 3pm), with 5-storey Disney characters, makes its way along Main Street, through **Liberty Square** and **Frontierland**. Most evenings (at 8 or 9pm in summer with an extra show at 11pm on special nights) the SpectroMagic electrical parade follows the same route. It's alight with fibre-optic and laser effects, huge holographic images, and a blaze of colour, tempting photographers to try to do it justice. The Plaza, the hub of the Magic Kingdom, is one popular spot for watching. Another is Town Square — especially the **Walt Disney World Railroad Station** and steps — which is better if you plan to leave the park right after the parade goes by.

The best viewing places tend to be grabbed early, but securing them would be hardly worth the use of your precious time on a short visit. A small fortune in **fireworks** goes up in smoke at 10pm on those summer evenings when the Magic Kingdom is open late.

tually work — for example, the haunted ballroom scene where several ghostly couples whirl in an eternal waltz. The answer? Holography. The journey finishes with the ghosts playing a trick so clever that it would be a shame to spoil the surprise.

Fantasyland

Walt Disney's dream was to make fairy stories come to life. In those terms, this land is really the heart of the Magic Kingdom. The toytown buildings are straight out of Disney's classic films.

Several times a day, an energetic musical show hits the **Castle Forecourt Stage** at the edge of the Plaza. Many of the songs are Disney hits, and Disney characters join in with the dancing.

Don't expect any thrilling rides inside **Cinderella Castle** itself, but spare a moment to inspect the fine mosaics that depict the fairytale, taken from scenes from the famous 1950 Disney film. Even if you don't eat here, walk up the ceremonial staircase to King Stefan's Banquet Hall. To make it a landmark, the castle was built to over 55 metres (180 feet), more than double the height of its predecessor, Sleeping Beauty Castle in California's Disneyland, which almost disappeared as trees grew up around it.

Through the archway and straight ahead, the most traditional ride in the Kingdom, **Cinderella's Golden Carousel**, is a merry-go-round of 90 galloping horses. Take a careful look: this is a genuine old fairground ride, meticulously restored and adapted. Next to it, under the cable cars of the Skyway, duplicates of **Dumbo the Flying Elephant** circle and soar; riders have control of the height. Dumbo's manager, Timothy Mouse, directs operations from the top of a ball in the centre. This ride is a hit with the very young and, even though it is not a long trip, limited capacity means long waits at peak periods.

On the left through the castle archway, you might miss the cinema presenting **Magic Journeys**, a 3-D film that is viewed through polarizing glasses. The realism is remarkable; it's hard not to duck as various objects fly towards you. Speaking of ducks, Donald co-stars with the special effects in the part-live, part-animated action. Left again and round the corner you'll find yourself at the entrance to **Peter Pan's Flight**, inspired by J. M. Barrie's book and the Disney film of 1953.

A silver-and-gold pavilion is home to the charming **It's a Small World**, "the happiest cruise that ever sailed." Everyone smiles at the hundreds of singing, dancing dolls dressed in folk costumes from every corner of the globe. The ride is always in demand, but as upwards of 30 boats run at any one time, the lines move relatively quickly.

In the Fantasyland **Lagoon**, Captain Nemo takes you in his submarine *Nautilus* in the **20,000 Leagues Under the Sea** adventure. If you've read the book or seen the Disney live-action film, you'll remember the attack of the giant squid, and Nemo playing the organ. If there's a long waiting time (and the queue does move slowly), come back after dark, when the special effects — artificial reefs, polar ice, and the lost city of Atlantis — are even more striking.

In the theme-park world, you can be anyone or anything that you want.

Based on Disney's enormously popular feature film, **Legend of the Lion King** incorporates scenes from the movie, animated special effects, and unusual puppetry recalling the show's Broadway theater version. Fans of the musical will enjoy Elton John's Academy Award-winning tunes, as well as narration by none other than Whoopi Goldberg.b

Snow White and the Seven Dwarfs was Disney's first full-length animated feature film, and when it was released some of it was considered to be too frightening for very small children. The same might be true of the ride **Snow White's Adventures**, in which your wagon rolls through the dark forest as the Wicked Witch tries to waylay you in between attempts to catch Snow White. The addition of new scenes featuring the endearing Snow White have made this attraction less terrifying for youngsters.

The last two rides in Fantasyland are at the far end, past the boarding point for the submarines. The reckless Mr. Toad stole a car, so the story goes in *The Wind in the Willows*, and drove it on a mad journey through the English countryside. **Mr. Toad's Wild Ride** gives you the chance to join him in a blend of ghost train and the Keystone Cops, dicing with disaster at every turn. The very young and nervous might be scared.

In the giant, whirling tea-cups of the **Mad Tea Party** you at least have some control: you can make them spin faster or slower. The idea originated from the Disney animated film of 1951, not directly from the Lewis Carroll book *Alice in Wonderland*. The ride itself is a variation on the Whip, an old fairground favourite and, like the Dumbo the Flying Elephant ride is designed for only small numbers of people at one time.

Mickey's Toontown Fair

When the ageless Mouse surprisingly reached a 60th birthday in 1988, the first all-new land to be added to the Magic Kingdom was opened to commemorate the event. Then called Mickey's Starland, its purpose was to offer everyone a chance to meet their favorite Disney stars — Donald Duck, Minnie, and of course the main Mouse himself. During Disney World's 25th Anniversary in 1996, Starland was rechristened as Micky's Toontown Fair, and the colorfully striped circus tents today offer youngsters short animated films, a miniature roller coaster, and plenty of star-studded photo opportunities.

The best way to get here is by taking the Walt Disney World Railroad from Town Square or from the Frontierland Station.

Mickey's Country House is set up like a museum of his career. You'll get an intimate glimpse into Mickey's private life, discovering his adorable baby pictures and a photo of Minnie in his bedroom. In the kitchen, cartoon cohorts Donald and Goofy have splattered paint all about during a rushed remodeling contest. Through the back door, you'll find Mickey in the **Judge's Tent** signing autographs

Minnie's Country House allows the curious to tour her office, crafts room, and kitchen. Listen to her answering machine, bake a quick cake, and look in the refrigerator. If you're lucky, you can catch her in her gazebo.

Admire the winning entries to the Toontown Fair in the **Toontown Hall of Fame,** among them plump pumpkins and handsome lima beans. Still more cartoon characters are on hand here to greet the public, and a large shopping area sells all manner of Disney paraphernalia.

The adventurous may wander over to **Goofy's Wiseacre Farms,** where **The Barnstormer** awaits. This small roller-coaster in the form of biplanes wreaks havoc when it plows through Goofy's barn.

Other attractions at Toontown Fair include **Donald's Boat,** the *Miss Daisy*, which sports a number of leaks and gives everyone a chance to cool off; the **Toontown Farmer's Market,** where you can shop for fresh-baked confections; and **Toon Park,** a glade with foam animal sculptures where kids may mount all manner of spongy beasts before checking out the interactive lily pads.

Tomorrowland

This is the end of our clockwise journey through the lands of the Magic Kingdom, a simple turn to the right if you've walked straight down Main Street.

Tomorrowland was completely overhauled in 1995 to turn it into a truly modern view of the future. Gone is the staid decor of the 1970s: the new Tomorrowland has been spruced up with whirligigs, flying doodads, and whimsical architecture, giving the sector a definite science-fiction look.

Mission to Mars, a simulated flight to the red planet, has been replaced by a new adventure featuring teleportation and an alien monster. There is another star attraction for those who are fearless — Space Mountain — and a mixture of rides appealing to various ages.

Young children will enjoy driving the cars of the **Grand Prix Raceway** around the twisting track. With an accelerator and brake, they have control of speed up to a modest maximum, but rails keep them mostly on one line — the steering wheel is redundant.

In place of the former Circle-Vision 360-degree film presentation, Disney has now installed the **Timekeeper,** a film experience in which viewers ride along with Jules Verne on a time machine. The old Star Jets still whirl around a rocket-shaped tower, but the ride is now called **Astro Orbiter**, and rotating planets have been installed on the top. A new entry also features space-age devices.

Takeflight, which will reopen after refurbishment in the fall of 1998, won't be altered. It traces the history of aviation through aircraft models up to full size, wide-screen footage of stunts, a world tour, and visions of the future. **Carousel of**

Progress, first shown at the 1964–65 New York World's Fair, has had some new figures added and one scene reworked. The outdoor theatre, which stages musicals, has been renamed the **Galaxy Palace Theater**.

The most dramatic new attraction in Tomorrowland is **Alien Encounter**, which employs tactile sensations in a ride that might be a bit scary for the young set. Viewers sit in a round theatre, in the centre of which is set a huge glass tube — ostensibly a teleportation machine. The process of teleportation is demonstrated to the audience, but something goes wrong, and instead of a person, a terrifying alien is transported into the tube. He breaks loose, the lights go out, and you can hear the fierce creature flapping around and

---

A Few Tips

- Dress is ultra-casual, but visitors must not go barefoot or bare-chested in the theme parks.
- Despite the clever layout, you'll be doing quite a lot of walking and standing, so wear your most comfortable clothing, especially shoes, and watch out for sunburn.
- Guests may not bring their own food and drink into the theme parks. There are plenty of places to eat inside.
- Most attractions forbid the use of flash photography.
- If you want to leave and return (even just to go to your car), be sure to have your hand stamped at the exit. You'll need your ticket as well.
- Carry some cash for fast food and drinks. Only sit-down restaurants accept credit cards.
- Smoking is not allowed anywhere in the attractions, or in the queues or waiting areas. Restaurants have smoking and non-smoking sections.
- If you hire a pushchair (stroller), tie a bright piece of clothing to it, or when you leave it someone may take it by mistake. Then you'll have an ethical dilemma: whether to take someone else's.

---

even devouring a victim. It's all good fun, though probably too alarming for young children.

Several of the rides remain virtually unchanged. **Space Mountain**, a roller coaster in the dark, is one of the Magic Kingdom's most popular attractions. However, you aren't allowed on the ride if you have neck or back problems, if your height is less than 1.10 metres (44 inches), or if you are pregnant. All kinds of things — glasses, handbags, and hats — have been recovered from the bottom of the ride.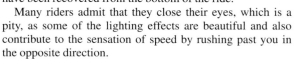

Many riders admit that they close their eyes, which is a pity, as some of the lighting effects are beautiful and also contribute to the sensation of speed by rushing past you in the opposite direction.

You can change your mind while you're waiting, and take a less harrowing ride on the **Tomorrowland Transit Authority**, a soothing. six-minute loop around the perimeter of Tomorrowland. Representing the future of mass transit, this electromagnetically-powered train emits no pollutants. Board at Rockettower Plaza.

The EPCOT Center

Most people would guess that EPCOT is an acronym, but few could say what it stands for. Walt Disney himself conceived the idea of an "Experimental Prototype Community of Tomorrow" with one scheme comprising a huge transparent dome, sealing in a whole city of progress. Early in the planning, several international pavilions, intended for a site next to the Magic Kingdom, became the centre of EPCOT's World Showcase. Then Future World took off when large U.S. corporations became excited by the concept and Exxon and AT&T (led by General Motors) signed on as sponsors.

EPCOT has two entrances: the main one near Spaceship Earth — that's the great white "golfball" that is visible for miles around — and International Gateway in the World Showcase, intended mainly for those guests coming in from EPCOT resorts.

If you come by Disney bus, they'll drop you near the main entrance. The Disney monorail system links EPCOT with the Magic Kingdom and its resorts by way of a change of train at the Travel and Transportation Center (TTC).

From the EPCOT resorts — the Swan, Dolphin, Board Walk, and Yacht and Beach clubs — it's only a short walk or ride on a shuttle tram to International Gateway between the pavilions of France and the United Kingdom.

If you come by car, you'll be directed to a place in the huge parking area. Rows are numbered and the zones are named, but in case you forget whether you're in Communication or Imagination, write down the location. Parking is free for guests who are staying in Disney-owned accommodation. Others should keep their parking ticket, as it is valid for the whole day.

You'll need to buy a one-day ticket or a four- or five-day pass. Pushchairs and wheelchairs can be rented, and if in doubt, take into account the long distances you will have to walk to see both of the EPCOT worlds; jokers say the letters really stand for "Every Person Comes Out Tired."

The park is in the shape of a figure eight, aligned north to south. The main entrance is at the north end.

Future World

This half of the figure eight illustrates the wonders of science and communications and the achievements of technology, both now and with predictions for the future. In recent years changes here have begun to reflect greater awareness of environmental concerns. The human dimension is also more in evidence, with an increased emphasis on biology and medicine, health and exercise.

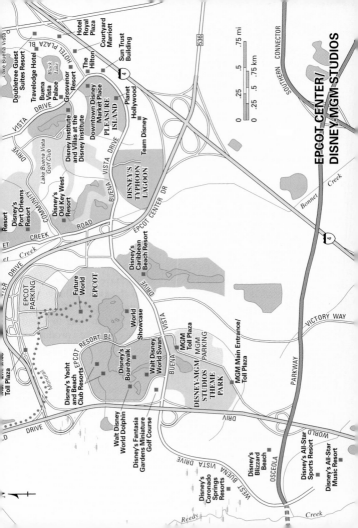

EPCOT CENTER/ DISNEY-MGM-STUDIOS

0   .25   .5   .75 mi
0   .25 .5 .75 km

Hotel Royal Plaza
Courtyard Marriott
Sun Trust Building
HOTEL PLAZA BL
Doubletree Guest Suites Resort
Lake Buena Vista
Travelodge Hotel
The Hilton
Buena Vista Palace
Black Lake
Grosvenor Resort
Planet Hollywood
Downtown Disney Market Place
Disney Institute and Villas at the Disney Institute
PLEASURE ISLAND
Team Disney
VISTA DRIVE
BUENA VISTA DRIVE
DRIVE
Lake Buena Vista Golf Club
Disney's Typhoon Lagoon
Resort
Disney's Port Orleans Resort
Disney's Old Key West Resort
COMMUNITY DRIVE
CREEK
EPCOT CENTER DR
ET Creek
ROAD
EPCOT CENTER DRIVE
Disney's Caribbean Beach Resort
Bonnet Creek
SOUTHERN CONNECTOR
536
4
4
EPCOT PARKING
Future World
EPCOT
World Showcase
ER DRIVE
MONORAIL
Toll Plaza
EPCOT RESORT BL
BUENA VISTA DRIVE
Disney's Yacht and Beach Club Resorts
Disney's Boardwalk
Walt Disney World Swan
Walt Disney World Dolphin
Disney's Fantasia Gardens Miniature Golf Course
MGM Toll Plaza
DISNEY-MGM STUDIOS THEME PARK
MGM/ MGM PARKING
MGM Main Entrance/ Toll Plaza
VICTORY WAY
PARKWAY
DRIVE
D DRIVE
WORLD DRIVE
WEST BUENA VISTA DRIVE
OSCEOLA
Disney's Coronado Springs Resorts
Disney's Blizzard Beach
Disney's All-Star Sports Resort
Disney's All-Star Music Resort
Reedy   Creek

Landmark of Future World, **Spaceship Earth** is a 55-metre (180-foot) "geosphere" made up of over 14,000 aluminium and plastic triangles. The "skin" is designed so that any rainwater falling on it is funnelled inside and piped away to the lake. The ride is one of EPCOT's most popular and, uniquely, the queue starts to form before 9:00 A.M. Queues tend to be long all day, this being the first attraction that most people see. You may want to wait until evening.

The **Spaceship Earth Ride** spirals upwards, tracking the history of human communication from cave drawings and Egyptian hieroglyphics to the invention of printing. It climbs onto the advent of film, radio, television, and satellite, then through an awe-inspiring "star field" and distant views of our home planet before making a backwards descent. Near the sphere's supporting pillars, **Earth Station** is the main information and restaurant reservation centre.

The twin curved buildings that used to house Communi-Core, a sector of interactive exhibits, have been completely refurbished and enlarged. Between the two buildings is a new computerized fountain that jets columns of water as high as 46 metres (150 feet) into the air in time to music. This sector, now called **Innoventions**, features products at the cutting edge of new development, and includes commercial companies exhibiting their goods.

Visitors can see, touch, and test out the latest goods — including some that have not yet reached the shops. The exhibits include computers, medical products, kitchen gadgets, home furnishings, and exercise gear. The exhibits change constantly as new ideas and products are developed, so this is a place in which you can really browse through the future.

Innovations West is geared more for the younger crowd, with massive, state-of-the-art exhibits from Sega, IBM, and

Test the limits of your imagination at Space Mountain.

others. There are also on display more than 200 interactive video games to tempt visitors of all ages.

Innovations East appeals more to adults, with technological gizmos from General Electric and Honeywell. For the home, there is a device that allows you to control by phone the lights and other domestic appliances. Also not to be missed are the bathroom innovations such as toilet lids that automatically raise and lower.

The Pavilions of Future World

The seven pavilions form a circle, with gaps on the north side (the main entrance) and the south (where the two worlds of EPCOT join). To get to the first pavilion you should cut through Innoventions and keep going to the left.

Ellen's Energy Adventure: Featuring Ellen DeGeneres, the star of the television situation comedy *Ellen*, as the taped hostess, this attraction tells the story of energy from prehistoric days when oil was being formed to energy sources of the future. The innovative seating area begins in the midst of three enormous 70mm screens, then divides into separate cars that move through dioramas and exhibition rooms. Trekking through the primordial ooze, you bump into ravenous brontosaures and swooping pterodactyls, only to emerge decidedly in the 20th century, before another set of 70mm screens in Theater II. Here Ellen learns about the energy challenges currently facing our world, and our high-tech solutions to increasingly scarce resources. Finally you return to the initial theatre to see Ellen reign as champion of the television quiz show *Jeopardy*, using her new-found energy knowledge.

Wonders of Life: In the Met Life Corporation's gold-domed building, Wonders of Life focuses on biology and health. In **Body Wars**, you are "miniaturized" to the size of a blood cell and propelled on a reckless ride through the human cardiovascular system to fight a bacterial infection. As in the popular Star Tours trip at Disney-MGM Studios (see page 52), you're strapped into a flight simulator facing a screen on which pictures are synchronized with the cabin's movements. Boarding restrictions apply on this ride.

Cranium Command takes a hilarious look at how a 12-year-old boy's mind and body learn to cooperate through a hyperactive day, harangued by a military martinet called "General Knowledge." Celebrities act the parts of the left and right sides of the boy's brain, and his heart, stomach, and adrenal gland.

The Making of Me explores all the wonders of pregnancy and birth by combining romance, cartoon spermatozoa competing to reach the egg, and remarkable live film of a developing foetus. It's all very sensitively done, though there is a notice warning people to use their discretion in deciding whether they should view it.

Goofy About Health has Disney's cartoon character appearing on seven screens to demonstrate the do's and don'ts of healthy living. In live shows staged throughout the day, the witty and quick-thinking **AnaComical Players** improvise skits involving the audience.

At the **Met Lifestyle Revue** you punch details into a computer and check on your own health habits. **Coach's Corner** gives you a chance to demonstrate your swing at golf, your tennis stroke, or your baseball skills, and analyses your game. Or try out **Wondercycles**, exercise machines with a programmed video tour and read-outs of your speed and the number of calories you've used — which turns out to be remarkably few.

Last but not least, **Sensory Funhouse** takes the old fairground idea of distorting mirrors and extends it to all the senses, with hands-on (as well as eyes- and ears-on) exhibits.

Horizons: The whole of the Horizons building is taken up by one of EPCOT's most complex rides. On a trip through the future imagined by visionary writers and film-makers of the past, we find that most of their predictions look comical to us now. After viewing electrifying images of today's world in micro- and macro-photography, projected on a giant OmniSphere screen, push a button to choose which landscape — desert, underwater, or space — you want to speed through in order to end the journey.

Test Track: General Motors has totally revamped the World of Motion pavilion, which used to take visitors on a placid chair ride through the history of cars and other forms of transportation. The new pavilion, which opened in 1997, features a new ride, Test Track, which takes top honors as the longest and fastest in the theme park (with the cars approaching 100 km/h (65 mph). The 2-km- (1-mile-) long ride is based on a car test track, and leads both inside and outside the pavilion. Sitting six in a car, riders experience a five-minute race around a track of banked turns which takes them through wind, cold and heat, and even a simulated crash.

In **Transcenter**, you can sit in a whole range of the sponsors' cars. The message that the internal combustion engine is still the way forward is reinforced in a screen debate.

Odyssey Complex: Next to the Test Track, the Odyssey Complex houses the First Aid and Baby Care Center, and a Lost Children desk. Here, you have reached the crossover of EPCOT's figure-eight layout. You can make a detour into World Showcase, on foot or in one of the boats that cross the lagoon, but in this guide we continue round the circle of Future World. If you want to do the same, cut through Innoventions West, or take the walkway by the lagoon.

Journey into Imagination: Kodak's Journey into Imagination, in its blue glass double pyramid, suggests that almost anything is possible as you take a 14-minute ride through a world of wild ideas. **Magic Eye Theater** shows the 3-D movie **Honey, I Shrunk the Audience,** easily one of the most popular attractions at EPCOT. This film demonstrates the "shrinking" effects of the two films starring Rick Moranis, who plays an inventor at the helm of an out-of-control shrinking machine. The 3-D effects bring the action to within inches of your face, and you'll see people reaching out to touch. Upstairs, **The Image Works** is a "playground of the future," with interactive games, light and sound trickery, and hands-on video screens. There's a **Cameras and Film** shop near the Magic Eye Theater. Outside the *Honey, I Shrunk the Audience* show take a look at the fascinating "jumping" fountains, where the water jumps all by itself from one pool to another.

The Land: This pavilion (by Kraft General Foods) actually grows some of the food used in the park's own restaurants, such as the hot, red peppers in Mexico's San Angel Inn. **Living with The Land**, a boat trip, cruises through greenhouses set up to simulate tropical rainforest, desert, and the American plains, and past a traditional farmstead.

If you are especially interested in the above, take the one-hour **The Land Backstage Tour** instead — you walk through the same areas and learn about them in more detail. Numbers are limited, however, so make reservations early at the **Green Thumb Emporium** through the gift shop near Farmer's Market food court. Starting every half-hour, the walk is guided by one of the farmers ("professional agricultural staff" in Disney parlance) who explains some of the techniques.

Food Rocks Theater offers Audio-Animatronic rock and roll, featuring such noted performers as Füd Wrapper (based on rapper Tone Loc), the Peach Boys (singing "Good Nutrition"), and the Refrigerator Police ("Every Bite You Take"). Some of the real musicians have re-recorded their own tunes with new lyrics about healthy eating.

The 70mm **Circle of Life** theater features a 15-minute motion picture bases on characters from **The Lion King,** as Simba the lion, Timon the meerkat, and Pumbaa the warthog deliver a message about land use and the environment.

The Living Seas: Housed in a building shaped rather like an octopus, United Technologies Corporation sponsors this experience, which claims to have the biggest saltwater fish-tank in the world — over 18 million liters (5 million U.S. gallons). Next to an imitation coral reef live 80 species of tropical fish, sharks, dolphins, and Florida's famous manatee.

You zigzag past a history of underwater exploration to board a brief ride through a submerged transparent tunnel. Then you can take as long as you like at the dual-level **Sea Base Alpha**, watching the fish and sea mammals close-up, as well as divers working in the tank. Experiments taking place are explained by the scientists, and you can even try on a diving suit. At the **Coral Reef Restaurant** you can sit and face the reef itself.

World Showcase

The second "circle" of EPCOT, around the shores of a lagoon, celebrates the culture and cuisine of 11 nations. Each "country" is housed in a microcosm of its own striking architecture, and naturally sets out to sell itself with the best possible image. In this guide we take a clockwise tour.

Mexico: An ancient Mayan pyramid looks as if it might eventually suffer the fate of its original brethren in Yucatán and be overgrown by jungle greenery. All is cool, dark, and mysterious inside, with beautiful displays of priceless pre-Columbian treasures.

At the back of the building, a boat trip on *El Rio del Tiempo* (the River of Time) meanders past an erupting volcano, a film of an Aztec ceremony, an animated fiesta, and market-stall traders which are all convincing enough to have you making an offer. Another film proclaiming the tourist attractions of Mexico is followed by an ingenious fibre-optic "firework display."

Norway: Oslo's 14th-century Akershus Castle, a turf-roofed cottage, a traditional wooden stave church, and 17th-century harbourside houses from Bergen inspired the buildings for the Norway pavilion.

Don't miss **Maelstrom**, the popular and thrilling Viking longboat voyage which takes you on a trip through Norway's myths and legends. Along the way you'll meet threatening three-headed trolls and then sliding backwards down a cataract to the churning water of a North Sea storm. You disembark in a little port and see *The Spirit of Norway*, an inspirational short film that will make you want to go there. A display entitled "To the Ends of the Earth" is housed inside, showing some relics of Nansen's and Amundsen's famous expeditions to both North and South poles.

China: Another fine collection of replica buildings centres on Beijing's circular Temple of Heaven, the perfect setting for showing a Circle-Vision 360° film travelogue, the *Wonders of China*. Along the Great Wall and down the Yangtze River, and from Lhasa to Shanghai, you will see more of China in just 19 minutes than a visit could cover in a year.

The business of fun and adventure is something that needs to be taken seriously.

Germany: Food and rural cosiness is the scene in the German pavilion, where the main attraction is the **Biergarten**, with plenty of German food and loud, rousing music. For all the folksy image, the little toytown-like shops are engaged in real business: chocolates at **Süssigkeiten**, wines in the **Weinkeller**, and **Volkskunst** for those crafts and souvenirs that everyone takes home from Germany, from beer steins to cuckoo clocks.

Italy: Beautifully detailed replicas of the Doge's Palace and the Campanile recreate a miniature of St. Mark's Square in Venice, complete with gondola moored at the lakeside. Other buildings, statues, and gardens round the piazza are based on originals from various regions of Italy. A troupe of strolling comic actors and singers often pulls a crowd and talks some of them into performing, with predictably dire results.

The United States: You won't be surprised to find the host nation taking centre spot at the head of EPCOT's lagoon. Presented by two potent U.S. corporations, American Express and Coca Cola, two centuries of American history pass painlessly by in no more than half an hour in *The American Adventure* (a name often given to the whole pavilion). It uses some of the most advanced Audio-Animatronic figures yet made, headed by hosts Mark Twain and Benjamin Franklin.

Japan: The well-groomed gardens with their waterfalls, little bridges, and carved stone lanterns make a perfect retreat from the world around. The tall, stepped pagoda and "flying roof" palace are based on historic temples of Nara and Kyoto. As well as four restaurants, the pavilion houses the **Bijutsukan Gallery** of traditional and contemporary art.

Morocco: As the only representative here of the Arab and Islamic worlds, Morocco took its responsibility very seriously. Moroccan workers were sent to construct perhaps the most authentic of all the World Showcase buildings. The superb tilework and intricate detail are not so much replicas as a living art form — look out especially for the **Koutoubia Minaret**, a beautifully detailed prayer tower, and a reproduction of the Nejjarine fountain. The **Gallery of Arts and History** displays art treasures, intricate embroidery, and jewellery. In a re-creation of an ancient kasbah, artisans work with brass and silver.

France: Not surprisingly, gastronomy is the main theme here, and three superstar chefs (Bocuse, Lenôtre, and Vergé) are advisors to the restaurants. The big, five-screen 18-minute travelogue *Impressions de France* will also whet your appetite for a trip. If you think you know the country already, think again! You'll hardly mistake the mini-Eiffel Tower for the real thing, but the rest of the architecture is a real *tour de force* in 19th-century Parisian style. With mansard roofs, pavement cafés, and the banks of a waterway a little like the Seine, it catches the atmosphere better than by trying to be an exact replica.

International Gateway: As EPCOT began operations, it made sense to add quicker access to the park. "Trams" run to and from the Swan and Dolphin, Board Walk, and Yacht and Beach Clubs, but the walk along the waterfront path only takes a few minutes.

The United Kingdom: Somehow designers have managed to compress a composite English village-town-city, with a dash of Scotland and Wales, too, into a living travel brochure. Architectural styles ranging from early Tudor to high Victorian are included, in convincing detail. The **Rose & Crown** pub feels quite like home to British visitors — and the beers are quite authentic (but cold and pasteurized to suit American tastes and laws).

Canada: Inspired by the Château Laurier in Ottawa, Hôtel du Canada is the landmark. Massive though it looks, even close-up it's really not much bigger than a good-sized house. *O Canada!* is a Circle-Vision 360° film that takes you from coast to coast through the great outdoors. You'll wish you had 360° eyes, too, as the pictures taken by a nine-camera battery from helicopters, planes, sleds, and canoes surround you. So does the sound, most sensationally in the ice-hockey match.

A musical moment at the Norway pavilion.

Disney-MGM Studios Theme Park

Celebrating the American love affair with movies, this combination theme park, production set, and educational center opened in

1989. Probably more like 1930 Hollywood than Hollywood ever was, its Art-Deco streets lead you along to real and replica sets. They really do make film and television programmes here, as you'll see through the windows into the working studio areas. There's plenty of audience participation, for all ages, in the attractions and street "happenings."

If you come by car, signs are easy to follow from the I-4 or US 192 highways. Parking is free for guests at Disney-owned accommodation, if they show their resort ID card. Others should keep their parking ticket — it's valid all day. If you are staying at one of the EPCOT resorts, you can come by waterbus. Check when the park closes; this varies from 7:00 P.M. onwards, occasionally as late as midnight during the summer months.

Touring Disney-MGM

Once through the gates, you may feel as if you're in a California dream, but even if there is an impromptu show going on in the street, don't linger. Similarly, you can check out shops and buy a snack later. Instead, walk straight ahead down **Hollywood Boulevard** towards **Sunset Plaza**. On the right you'll see a huge board chalked with the latest information on times of shows and special events.

In this guide, we follow a route which roughly circles the park in a clockwise direction, but you'll need to be flexible. If you want to ride Star Tours (see page 52), you'd do well to go straight there at opening time, and then make for the Indiana Jones Stunt Spectacular (see page 52) for the first session of the day. After that, you might get quickly into the queue for one of the behind-the-scenes tours (see page 53). By the time you come out, the queues will have built up at all the popular attractions, but at least you'll have had a head start.

Check the schedule of the **Theater of the Stars**, now situated in Sunset Boulevard, for the times of the live stage musical based on Walt Disney Pictures' animated hit, ***Beauty and the Beast***. You can see some of it without waiting for a seat, if you're pressed for time. Make a note of the times of another show not far away on Sunset Plaza. Based on another Disney animated feature, it brings to life the story of the *Little Mermaid* in a delightful musical production — the song *Under the Sea* won the film an Oscar. Combining live performance and puppets as well as film clips, it takes place in an undersea grotto with a curtain of water and other special effects. Realism extends to spraying the audience gently and filling the theatre with bubbles, so cover your camera.

Meanwhile, in the middle of Sunset Plaza, the **Star Today** (a major or minor name from films or TV) will turn up periodically — details are given in the Entertainment Schedule.

The Rides

In Sunset Boulevard, a new sector of Disney-MGM created in 1995, stands one of the tallest structures in Walt Disney World. Resembling an old Hollywood hotel, the structure houses a new ride, **Twilight Zone Tower of Terror.** Guests ride to the top of the building, but suddenly the elevator breaks loose and falls 13 stories. It's a sudden and — for a few seconds — terrifying fall. Screams echo all the way down the boulevard.

The **Chinese Pagoda**, Sunset Plaza, is a full-size replica of **Hollywood's Chinese Theater**, where stars' foot- and handprints are set in cement — here they've done the same. Inside, the 20-minute **Great Movie Ride** is a tribute to some of the landmark productions of a hundred years of film-making. Your seat moves on a twisting track through vivid scenes from *Casablanca, The Wizard of Oz, Raiders of the Lost Ark,* and dozens more classics, with life-size Audio-Animatronics figures of stars and some realistic special effects (perhaps too realistic for very small children).

While you wait to get into the **ABC Sound Studio**, you'll see a video featuring *101 Dalmatians*, a recent addition to Disney-owned ABC's Saturday morning cartoons. In the show itself, the audience help to add the sound effects to a scene of salesman Chevy Chase arriving at a haunted house, with hilarious results. A 15-minute show follows, documenting Disney sound master Jimmy McDonald, who took over as Mickey Mouse's voice when Walt Disney gave up the honour in 1946.

SuperStar Television is a live re-creation of the making of some of TV's all-time hit shows such as *I Love Lucy*, *The Golden Girls,* and *General Hospital*, with some of the audience taking part. Clever cutting makes the final footage feature them interacting with the real stars, past and present.

Check the schedules and go quickly to the vast open-air theatre for the **Indiana Jones Stunt Spectacular**, which occurs several times a day. Generally you need to get here in advance of the start times. It's live, on three sets, and you can even join in — if you dare. "Extras" are chosen from the audience before the show, so be there early if you want to volunteer. Some sequences reveal "how it was done" in *Raiders of the Lost Ark* and *Indiana Jones and the Temple of Doom*. At the climax the scene explodes in sheets of flame.

At **Star Tours**, a battered *Starspeeder* space-craft with *Star Wars* characters C-3P0 and R2D2, as well as deranged robots at work, suggests that all might not be as smooth as the space travel agency claims. On board, you're welcomed by a loony captain, then the thrills begin as you experience the "virtual reality" of a runaway ride. The flight-simulator cabin is thrown around while graphic scenes of the hazards of flying through a comet's tail, an interstellar dog-fight, or along the streets of a hostile city are perfectly synchronized on the big screen in front of you. It's not for the very nervous — and there's a string of boarding restrictions. Jim Henson's **Muppet*Vision 3-D** sends flying objects right at you and surrounds you with special effects, fibre optics, and Audio-Animatronics figures of Muppet characters as well as "live" ones.

At **Honey, I Shrunk the Kids**, just as in the film of the same name in which a scientist accidentally miniaturizes his and the neighbours' children to the size of ants, you'll discover what it might be like to roam through a forest of 7.5-metre (25-foot) blades of grass and meet insects as big as a house. Small children can climb up "spiders' webs" and slide down tubes of foliage or a huge roll of discarded "film."

Behind-the-Scenes Tours

Try to go early to **The Magic of Disney Animation**, because you are more likely to see artists at work early in the day rather than at lunchtime or in the late afternoon. The starting point is just off Sunset Plaza behind Theater of the Stars, and

All the World's a Stage

It was a stroke of genius to call the people who work at Walt Disney World, all 34,000 of them, "cast members." This is the entertainment business, the reasoning goes, and just as certain rules apply to the acting profession, so do they here. The language reflects this; the cast wear "costumes," not uniforms, and they're kept in the "wardrobe," not the locker room. When they're in view of the visitors (the "guests"), they're "on stage" — and there's no smoking or drinking.

Actors and actresses would never wear the wrong sort of jewellery or make-up: nor do the Disney cast. No eyeliner or very bright lipstick for the women, no large earrings, a maximum of one ring per hand, and no "facial hair" for men (with one or two exceptions — after all, Walt himself had a moustache).

much of the tour is a self-guided walk, beginning with a short and hilarious film, *Back to Never Land*, a lesson in the basics of animation. With Walter Cronkite as the host and Robin Williams not quite ready to be animated, you will learn how a roughly sketched cartoon character is given life.

Next comes a real animation studio where you can take your time to move along, looking through the windows and over the shoulders of artists. You'll see each department — not all at work at any particular moment, but video-monitors along the way will explain — what goes on in each: developing the story, drawing the characters to convey movement and emotion, designing the special effects and backgrounds, carefully hand-painting the plastic "cels" (see page 23) and photographing them one-by-one. Last comes the editing, and as a finale you'll see special sequences from famous films including *Bambi* (Walt Disney once admitted it was his favourite), *101 Dalmatians,* and *Cinderella* in the Disney Classic Theater.

The best examples of the animator's art have now come to be recognized as modern classics, and connoisseurs pay high prices for them. Original "cels" once sold for a few dollars each, but they can now fetch several thousand dollars. In the **Animation Gallery** here you'll see examples on sale.

The afternoon is probably a good time to go on the excellent **Backstage Studio Tour**, beginning near the Little Mermaid show off Sunset Plaza. Departures are almost continuous for the 20-minute shuttle ride, taking you first through costuming and scene building, then past stored props and old cars, and even old aircraft. **Residential Street** is an outdoor set with some backless "houses" that may look familiar from films and TV shows (*The Golden Girls'* house, for example). Then, watch out! In **Catastrophe Canyon** you get a memorable look at the artificial floods, fires, and explosions that gave disaster movies their name. If you're sitting on the right side, you may get splashed, and on the left you definitely will, so cover your camera. Incidentally, it only takes 3½ minutes to recycle the 318,000 litres (70,000 gallons) of water and to have the catastrophic chain of events ready for a replay.

You can break off the tour at this stage, but if you're ready to go on, follow Roger Rabbit's pink, painted footsteps to **Inside the Magic: Special Effects and Production Tour**, a walking tour that takes from 45 minutes to an hour to complete. You'll see how hurricanes and sea battles are simulated in a tank, with a member of the audience as the hapless captain in one storm-tossed model. You also look down into three real working sets: Soundstages I-III. Check the Entertainment Schedule to see what may be going on, and which star personalities might be around.

In **Post-Production Editing and Audio**, the editors and sound engineers explain how they add the finishing touches, with a taped George Lucas lecturing side-by-side with his cohorts R2D2 and C-3PO. The tour finishes in the Walt Disney Theater with previews of Disney and Touchstone productions coming, in the time-honoured phrase, "to a theater near you."

You'll feel like you're on a New York street in this recreated scene at Disney's MGM studios.

The restaurants in Disney-MGM Studios are part of the show. **The Hollywood Brown Derby Grill**, near Theater of the Stars, has a Wall of Fame of caricatures, and talkalikes of the two famous gossip-column queens, Louella Parsons and Hedda Hopper, might well be at one of the tables. At **50's Prime Time Café** you can eat while vintage sitcoms play on television. The **Sci-Fi Dine-In Theater** serves up sandwiches while you sit in booths that look like 1950s convertibles and watch science-fiction B-movies from the same period.

Disney's Animal Kingdom

Opened in mid-1998, this extraordinary new theme park is the most expansive of the Disney domain: five times larger than the Magic Kingdom and almost twice the size of EPCOT, the Animal Kingdom stretches out to encompass the African savannah and stretches back in time to the age of Tyrannosaurus Rex.

The Oasis

As your point of entry into the wilderness, the Oasis offers a tranquil spot to prepare for wild safari adventures and miraculous time travel. Admire the exotic flora and fauna of a lush tropical garden here, with cool mists enshrouding idyllic waterfalls and pristine glades. Attentive visitors will find within the miniature landscape unusual animal life and startling, fragrant flowers.

Safari Village

Encircled by the **Discovery River,** this central station serves as an island gateway to the rest of the Animal Kingdom. The village is dominated by the 14-storey **Tree of Life,** the symbolic heart of the park which stretches 15 metres (50 feet) wide at its base. The tree is lavishly decorated with carvings of animal forms and African motifs. Within the tree one finds a digitally-enhanced theatre showing a 3-D animated film of life from the perspective of an insect. Paradoxically, from a bug's-eye point of view, the world seems much less confusing. Board the skiffs that ply the Discovery River, and row past the **Dragon Rocks** on an Odyssean voyage. You'll narrowly escape the clutches of mythical monsters, and will avoid plummeting into steaming geysers.

Dinoland U.S.A.

Devoted to everyone's favorite extinct creatures, this area of the park boasts the **Countdown to Extinction,** where you'll travel back 65 million years just in time to rescue a dinosaur from certain doom when a meteor crashes into the earth. In this attraction, more than two dozen animatronic creatures simulate the dinosaur realm, while computer-controlled motion effects and moving motion-simulator vehicles pitch you to and fro.

If you haven't seen enough of the fabled Tyrannosaurus Rex, Triceratops, or the wily Brachiosaurus, you may enjoy wandering down the **Cretaceous Trail,** a path devoted to the plants and animals of the dinosaur era. Deeper in the undergrowth lies the **Theater in the Wild,** a 1,500-seat amphitheater for live stage performances. Finally, the **Boneyard** playground offers a place for the young ones to dig for dinosaur bones and other fossils, in the manner of an open-air archaeological site.

Africa

Here the real adventure begins, just after passing through the **Harambe,** where an ancient baobab tree stands guard over the wildlife sanctuary. You'll learn that animals in the park were collected from around the world, carefully selected from those born in zoological parks, rescued from endangered habitats, or saved after being orphaned in the wild. Stop in at **Conservation Station** via the **Wildlife Express**

Train for more information about Disney's efforts to handle its prize collection responsibly, and meet the park's excellent veterinary staff.

Next, set off on the **Kilimanjaro Safaris,** where you'll prowl over 40 hectares (100 acres) of open land in search of adventure. The wildlife reserve is filled with varying terrain, from thick, densely wooded forests to picturesque rivers and rolling hills. Speaking of pictures, don't forget to bring along the camera, as you'll definitely be running into some breathtaking animal life. Riding in open-sided cars, you can virtually butt heads with elephants and pass just within a jaw's snap of hungry alligators. Thrills abound when some crafty elephant poachers happen on the scene, and a wild, dusty ride ensues.

Other attractions in Africa include the **Gorilla Falls Exploration Trail,** a stroll to the grounds of lowland gorillas, where it is also possible to view the hippopotamus tank from an underwater portal, and an aviary with many rare birds.

Creating the Magic

"Don't they mind being watched?" Everyone on the **Magic of Disney Animation** Tour wants to know how the artists feel, working under the gaze of thousands of visitors each day. The answer is apparently "yes and no." Loss of privacy is balanced by the fact that they are being acknowledged instead of hidden in a back room. Now there's no doubt the balance has succeeded: the 70 artists here created 15,000 drawings and eight months' work for both *Beauty and the Beast* and *Aladdin*.

"Have there been any advances in technique since Walt Disney's day?" Disney would recognize everything going on here, though the artists have a written script now, whereas Disney kept the story in his head. Changes are on the way, however, with the possibility of "paperless animation," modelling in 3-D on computer screens. The artists are ready: "It will allow us to be even more creative."

OTHER WALT DISNEY WORLD ATTRACTIONS

Note that during bad weather some of the waterparks such as Typhoon Lagoon and Wet 'n' Wild (see page 73) may close.

Typhoon Lagoon

Faced with the competition of other waterparks round Orlando, Disney responded with this one with its own car park, free to Walt Disney World Resort guests. Towels can be hired, and, unusually for Walt Disney World parks, you can take in your own food and drink (no alcohol or glass), though food is available at two restaurants.

The park is imaginatively landscaped: in this 22-hectare (56-acre) South Sea island setting you can forget you're miles inland: there's even a white-sand beach for basking, and plenty of trees for shade. The main attraction is the giant **wave generator** which sends perfect bodysurfing rollers up to 1.8 metres (6 feet) in height across the 1-hectare (2½-acre) blue lagoon every 90 seconds. Periodically it goes into a gentler mode, producing non-breaking waves — then a horn sounds a warning before the "big ones" start again.

Mount Mayday, rising 27 metres (90 feet) above the lagoon, has the wreck of a shrimp boat, the *Miss Tilly*, perched convincingly on its peak as if cast there by a passing tidal wave. Climb up the hill for the view, shielding your camera from the frequent waterspouts that erupt from *Miss Tilly*'s funnel.

From over 15 metres (50 feet) up the slope, a couple of giant water slides — **Humunga Kowabunga** — send you screaming at 50 km/h (30 mph) through a tunnel to plummet into the lagoon. It's not for very small children, and there are a number of other restrictions. You may like to work up to it by first trying one of the shorter slides which twist their way in and out of caves and waterfalls on the way to splashdown.

Each about 90 metres (300 feet) long, the *Jib Jammer, Rudder Buster*, and *Stern Burner* body slides will send you at a fairly rapid clip to your final plunge.

For a gentler ride you can hop on the rubber inner tubes through the white water cascades of **Mayday Falls** and **Keelhaul Falls**, or go four at a time down **Gangplank Falls**. If the queues have grown too long, pick up an inner tube at one of the collection points and let **Castaway Creek** float you gently along, circling the park and meandering through woods and grottoes. Free equipment is available for snorkelling over

---

Which Did You Miss?

It may save a lot of arguments, or start them, but here's a list of all the Walt Disney animated feature films.

1930s *Snow White and the Seven Dwarfs* (1937)

1940s *Pinocchio* (1940); *Fantasia* (1940); *Dumbo* (1941); *Bambi* (1942); *Saludos Amigos* (1943); *The Three Caballeros* (1945); *Make Mine Music* (1946); *Fun and Fancy Free* (1947); *Melody Time* (1948); *The Adventures of Ichabod and Mr. Toad* (1949)

1950s *Cinderella* (1950); *Alice in Wonderland* (1951); *Peter Pan* (1953); *Lady and the Tramp* (1955); *Sleeping Beauty* (1959)

1960s *One Hundred and One Dalmatians* (1961); *Sword in the Stone* (1963); *The Jungle Book* (1967)

1970s *The Aristocats* (1970); *Robin Hood* (1973); *The Many Adventures of Winnie the Pooh* (1977); *The Rescuers* (1977)

1980s *The Fox and the Hound* (1981); *The Black Cauldron* (1985); *The Great Mouse Detective* (1986); *Oliver and Company* (1988); *The Little Mermaid* (1989)

1990s *The Rescuers Down Under* (1990); *Beauty and the Beast* (1991); *Aladdin* (1992); *The Lion King* (1996); *Hercules* (1997)

Where does *Mary Poppins* fit in? Answer: it was one of Disney's mixtures of live action and animation, like *Song of the South*. This list includes only pure animation.

Shark Reef, an artificial coral reef but with shoals of *real* fish and even some small (and harmless) sharks as companions. For the very young, **Ketchakiddie Creek** has paddling pools, small slides, and fountains. If you forgot to bring swimwear, **Singapore Sal's** has a good selection, as well as sun protection cream, hats, and every other beach essential.

River Country

On Bay Lake near the Magic Kingdom, this is a longer-established waterpark than Typhoon Lagoon. It has fewer and smaller slides and no wave machine, but many people like its relaxed atmosphere. Towel rental is available.

Instead of a tropical theme, River Country is designed as a rustic "ole swimmin' hole." The thrills come from **Whoop 'n' Holler Hollow**, two long corkscrew waterslides which rush you out of the trees to splash into the giant pool. Or ride an inner tube down the **White Water Rapids**, stretch out on the sandy beach, and picnic at the tables (you can bring your own food and drink in, but no alcohol or glass).

Discovery Island

A little world of its own exists almost unnoticed in the middle of Walt Disney World, and few visitors ever find it. On this 4-hectare (11-acre) island in **Bay Lake**, you can roam almost at will amid hosts of real birds and animals. Fifty species of wild bird are regularly logged, with 100 more in aviaries.

Trails and boardwalks wind their way through the cunningly contrived landscape and the lush greenery. Along the way, you'll spot swans, ringtail lemurs, peacocks, golden lion tamarins and giant Galapagos tortoises. Many of the animals move around freely, though you are subtly separated from the alligators and crocodiles, and all the inhabitants feel so unthreatened by visitors that you can get very close.

Spend the day riding the waves and cooling off at Typhoon Lagoon.

This is an accredited zoological park, with a growing record of success in breeding endangered species of birds. It specializes in hornbills, and was the second zoo in North America to raise the rare rhinoceros hornbill. On arrival, take note of the time of the next **Bird Show**. In a humorous performance, several talking macaws show off.

Discovery Island is reached by boat from River Country, Fort Wilderness, the Contemporary Resort, and from the Magic Kingdom near the main entrance.

Blizzard Beach

Disney's newest waterworld takes a different approach to the waterpark theme — one that is decidedly chillier. This 26-hectare (66-acre) "ski resort" surrounds Mount Gushmore, which swimmers may mount via chair lift. "Liquid ice" slopes and water-filled toboggan runs offer the main attractions, while purportedly fresh-melted ice offers pleasant refreshment on humid Florida days.

Inner-tubers may idle along **Cross Country Creek**, an 800-metre (2,900-foot) trough encircling the entire park. **Snow Stormers** pitches its victims down three flumes that switch back through slalom-style gates. As the main attraction on Mt. Gushmore, the **Summit Plummet** simulates a ski-jump tower, from which the adventurous may face a nearly vertical drop to the base of the mountain. Approaching speeds of 86 km/h (55 mph), swimmers let loose screams of terror and pleasure.

Pleasure Island

This resort primarily provides entertainment in the form of nightclubs and discos and is covered in detail on pages 91-94.

OTHER ATTRACTIONS IN THE ORLANDO AREA

Universal Studios Florida

More than just a theme park, **Universal Studios Florida** is billed as the "biggest film and TV production facility east of Hollywood." Your feet will believe it after a whole day here, which you'll need to experience some thrilling rides and see a selection of shows. North of International Drive and signposted off the I-4 interstate highway, it's easy to find by car. As with all theme parks, make a note of where you leave your car.

Our suggestions on making the most of your time on page 22 generally apply here as well: try to arrive before the 9:00 A.M. opening hour, collect a guide leaflet and map at the gate, decide your priorities, and make your way quickly to one of the popular attractions to beat the rush. Towards the end of each day people take up positions for the evening **Dynamite Nights Stunt Spectacular**, an explosive show set on the lagoon with high-speed boat chases and plenty of firepower.

The park is divided into six areas — on the map at least. On the ground the distinction does not much matter. This guide takes them here in a roughly clockwise order, but the route you choose may be different as you head for your objectives. **The Front Lot**, near the main entrance, includes most of the administrative clutter and production information — what's happening in the studios or on the sets.

Production Central

Straight ahead down **Plaza of the Stars** and right where it starts at the crossroads is one of the big attractions of Production Central, the **Funtastic World of Hanna-Barbera**. The partnership of Bill Hanna and Joe Barbera created the ever-popular cartoon characters of the *Flintstones*, *Yogi Bear*, and *Scooby Doo* — you may see the characters outside greeting the fans. This ride is a flight simulator which takes you on a thrilling high-speed chase driven by Yogi Bear, who obviously hasn't yet passed his test. It's not as violent as some rides of this kind, and stationary seats are provided at the front for the very young or anyone who would prefer not be rocked around.

The **Production Tour** tram chugs past sets that may be familiar from television shows — take it if you need to sit down. The late king of suspense presents a bag of tricks in **Alfred Hitchcock's 3-D Theatre**, where scenes from *The Birds* or *Psycho* come straight at you. In the shop you can buy Bates Motel hand towels for your favourite guests. In **Nickelodeon Studios,** you can tour the working television studio where such favourites as *Double Dare*, *Nick Arcade*, and *Ren and Stimpy* are feverishly produced.

Hollywood, off to the right, is a 1950s street set in chrome and pastel. Among the shops and cafés selling Hollywood hats, sunglasses, and posters, one attraction — if you can call it that — is the **Gory Gruesome and Grotesque Horror Make-Up Show**. The name says it all.

More up-to-date is the **Terminator 2 3-D** extravaganza, a film and special-effects showcase in which 3-D images are projected onto fully 180° of 70mm action. The 12-minute

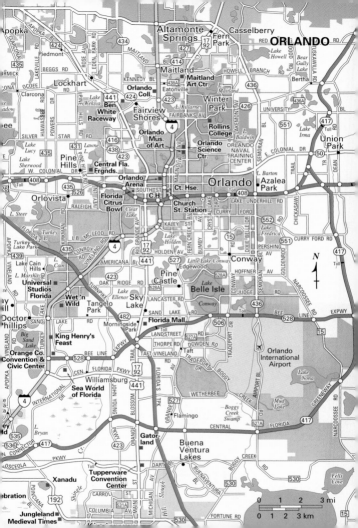

film is based, of course, on the blockbuster starring Arnold Schwarzenegger and Linda Hamilton, with some footage shot especially for this attraction.

The big new attraction is **Twister**, a gargantuan tunnel cloud based on the 1996 feature film. At five storeys in height, the cyclone will whip up immense volumes of air, while beating rains and a deafening roar complete the terrifying experience. This show will replace the long-running "Ghostbusters" attraction, trading the corny slime effects for a glimpse of natural disaster.

Meanwhile, out in the street, two Blues Brothers lookalikes pull up in their battered ex-cop car and do song and dance routines from the movie of the same name. In **Kongfrontation**, mighty King Kong, four storeys high, is rampaging through the city, swatting helicopters like flies. You are riding in a cable-car high above the street (don't ask why) when Kong attacks. Your life hangs by a thread. It's one of the biggest attractions in every way. Watch out for a time when the waiting line isn't too long, but don't miss it. You can also check out your reaction in a video playback afterwards.

You may have to tell yourself that it's only a plastic model.

San Francisco/Amity

Clustered round one end of the lagoon, San Francisco/Amity features sets of Fisherman's Wharf and Amity (*Jaws*) Harbour, snacks and seafood, and two outstanding attractions.

Earthquake — The Big One puts you in a San Francisco subway train, standing quietly at a station, when the quake begins. The roof falls in, chasms open in the platform, a truck from the street above slides down straight at you, and a tidal wave rolls in. The thrill measures 8.3 on the Richter scale.

The other big event here is *Jaws.* Yes, he's back (believe it or not) — and he's out to get you — just when you thought it was safe to go back in the water. Head off on the boat ride that almost ends in disaster as the 10-metre- (32-foot-) long great white shark attacks relentlessly (with a bit of help from sophisticated special effects and advanced technology).

After all this computer-controlled engineering, the **Wild, Wild, Wild West Stunt Show** is an old-fashioned contrast. It's fast and funny, with plenty of fist fights, gun fights, and stunts.

Expo-Center

The attractions here include **Animal Actors' Stage**, where some of the secrets of training dogs, cats, and birds to "act" are revealed and the trainees are put through their paces. Of course, they don't always do what's expected.

ET's Adventure is a gentle journey on a starbike to help ET's home planet, with some nice special effects. The last word in rides, however, with the biggest queues (so some people run straight here when the main gates open in the morning) is the dynamic and thrilling **Back to the Future**, which takes flight-simulator technology to new heights of realism and scale. While you are thrown about in DeLorean-shaped vehicles, the special effects and pictures are wrapped around you on monster hemispherical OmniMax screens.

Universal Citywalk

Opening in the fall of 1998, this new 4.5-hectare (12-acre) entertainment complex brings yet more exciting venues to

Ghostbusters has been one of the many spectacular stage shows at Universal Studios.

Universal's already bursting-at-the-seams attractions. City-Walk introduces a wealth of state-of-the-art spaces designed for hot live music, hip dancing, and gourmet celebrity restaurants, all based on the CityWalk complex at the Universal Studios Hollywood theme park in California. As you stroll around the lagoon and marvel at the true-to life cityscapes and labyrinthine waterways, you'll find lots to keep you busy. The best part of the deal: admission to CityWalk is free.

Among the attractions at CityWalk's vibrant promenade is **Bob Marley — A Tribute to Freedom,** a space devoted to the Jamaican musician and cultural icon.

The **Hard Rock Café Orlando** replaces the existing Hard Rock Café at Universal Studios Florida to become the world's largest, most rock-and-rollin' Hard Rock ever. This perennial attraction for lovers of burger-and-fries fare will sport the usual lavish decorations taken from the annals of popular music. The management has reserved a few extra touches, however, for their new flagship restaurant. The dining area is based on the architecture of the Forum in Rome, lending a distinctly classical ambiance to the affair. But lovers of grunge, funk, and pop need not despair: the site includes Hard Rock's first live-music venue, a 2,000-seat club boasting celebrity appearances. In keeping with the theme-park strategy, now you can successfully do dinner and a show all under one roof.

Two other entertainment venues in CityWalk include the Cineplex Odeon Megaplex, a monumental 16-screen, 5,000-seat theater complex sporting its own collection of restaurants and shops, and the E! Entertainment Television Production Center, a studio for the popular cable network which will open its doors to live audiences and offer live celebrity interviews. All of these attractions and more are nestled in among CityWalk's bustling strips of restaurants, jazz clubs, and music education sites. Don't miss special concerts hosted on the floating outdoor stage, which is tethered on CityWalk's 1.5-hectare (4-acre) lagoon.

Sea World

Marine parks are a Florida tradition and this is the biggest and best. **Shamu**, the friendly killer whale featured on the park's logo, is the star, but the various other attractions here could easily entertain and painlessly educate you all day. On the other hand, if you only have 2 or 3 hours, you can zip round and still see most of the highlights.

Near the south end of International Drive, Sea World has that first essential of Orlando theme parks, its own exit signs from the I-4 highway. At the gate, you'll be given an invaluable map marked with the times of each show, specially printed out as you enter. Use it to plan your visit. The distances between shows are not large and the shows are cleverly scheduled so you can easily move from one to another, fitting in one or two other attractions on your way. Near the entrance, you can change any money, rent lockers, wheelchairs, or pushchairs (strollers), naturally in the shape of dolphins, and ask about any special tours.

All over the park you can feed the dolphins, sea lions, and seals in their feeding pools.

The Shows

At **Whale and Dolphin Stadium**, you'll see the all the sorts of tricks that started the whole marine park phenomenon in Florida. Dolphins dance, somersault, do formation aerobatics, and shake flippers with children from the audience. Beluga whales, meanwhile, show that they're just as clever and almost as agile.

Aware of the doubts some people have about the ethics of keeping and training captive animals, Sea World emphasizes its role in conservation and research and backs several kinds of "green" causes. In the shows, the trainers go out of their way to stress the care that is taken of the cast.

Sea Lion and Otter Stadium is the venue for another of the more old-fashioned circus-type performances. Suppos-

---

Dilemma!

Which should you choose, Universal Studios Florida or Disney-MGM Studios?

Universal Studios is a lot bigger (which doesn't just mean more of the same), and there isn't the cosy, fairytale feeling of the Disney-MGM Studios. Also, fewer of the attractions are based on films made for the youngest audiences. In addition, the streets and sets of Universal Studios are on a grander scale, so there's more walking, but it does have some of the most thrilling rides you'll experience anywhere, though they might scare small children. Of course, true film fanatics will want to head for both Disney-MGM and Universal.

edly set in prehistoric times, it's fast and fun. The animals (plus a vast, hairy walrus) trick the cavemen, and convey an environmental message by picking up litter. **Sea World Theater** offers **The Mickey Finn Show,** a Dixie-style revue complete with banjos and piano. In the same location in the late afternoon, you can see a lights-and-music Water Fantasy show.

At **Shamu Stadium**, on the far side of the big lake, the star's extended family of killer whales entertain three times a day plus a "Night Magic" extra on certain evenings. It's the event not to miss at Sea World, and the big seating area fills up well before the start. The front 10 or 12 rows can expect to get splashed, if not completely soaked, by several hundred of the almost 20 million litres (6 million gallons) of salt water in the tank, so don't sit there if you value your camera or your hairstyle. As much as you'll admire the agility and gentleness of the whales, you'll also marvel at the skill and balance of their trainers, who get rocketed out of the water on the tip of a whale's nose.

The **Atlantis Waterski Stadium** faces the lake between Shamu Stadium and the entrance. The show, two or three times a day, is a themed acrobatic stunt and formation "ballet" on skis. If you've been to Cypress Gardens (see page 78), you'll know what to expect.

Other Attractions at Sea World

Some of the best things can be seen at practically any time of the day, mostly without a wait. In **Tropical Reef**, you stand in the cool darkness facing thousands of colourful fish in a huge, brilliantly lit aquarium, with separate tanks to keep incompatible species apart. Outside again, you can feed the harbour seals in their pool, and actually go and touch one of the stingrays in theirs.

On a hot and sticky Florida day you'll envy the inmates of **Penguin Encounter**, a large tank refrigerated to the Antarctic chill that penguins prefer. More than 4,000 kilograms (almost five tons) of snow fall here every day. As you drift by on a moving walkway, the glass walls let you see the residents hilariously marching and slipping on the rocks and ice, and then zooming away underwater.

Terrors of the Deep is not particularly terrifying, in spite of being surrounded by the largest collection in the world of various species of sharks as well as venomous fish such as lionfish, eels, and scorpion and puffer fish. You will be safely housed in a long, transparent underwater tunnel, with 15-centimetre- (6-inch-) thick walls.

A new water ride, **Journey to Atlantis,** sports a roller-coaster-style adventure based on the theme of the lost underwater city. Unsuspecting visitors clamber onto rickety boats, which begin to explore the ancient site. Lo and behold, the boats

At Universal Studios the "Back To the Future" ride takes immolation to new levels.

plunge 18 metres (60 feet) on a nearly vertical plummet to the depths of the ocean, only to surface after enduring hair-raising twists and turns through tidal waves. Along the way, holograms and LCD images bring the drama of the lost city to life.

A recent addition to Sea World is **Wild Arctic,** an exploration of the wonders of the world's northern latitudes. Visitors take a virtual helicopter ride in one of the three *White Thunder* chopper simulators, traveling far north to **Base Station Wild Arctic.** Along the way, notice the limitless vistas, rugged mountain peaks, and chilly marine life. When you reach the base, you'll step into an icy realm featuring 1,360-kilogram (3,000-pound) beluga whales, walruses, and, the star attraction, celebrity polar bears Klondike and Snow.

From underwater to high up in the sky, you can ride to the top of the needle-like 122-metre (400-foot) **Sky Tower**, which is worth it if only for the view (there's a small charge).

Two special **tours** also cost extra. On the 90-minute long **Backstage Explorations** you can learn about the care, training, feeding, and breeding of the 8,000 mammals, birds, and fish who reside here, and the 45-minute **Animal Training Discoveries** lets you see the actual "classes" going on.

Finally, Sea World has entered the business of "dinner-and-show," with a **Polynesian Luau** by the lake taking place in the early evening.

Wet 'n' Wild

You might have supposed that there are only a certain amount of ways you can climb steps, slide down, and splash into a shallow pool. Here they have thought of all those, and then some — there are now 14 different slides and rides. Right on International Drive (at Republic Drive, exit 30A south off the I-4 highway), Wet 'n' Wild is convenient to reach from the hotels in that area.

From gentle slopes perfect for a baby, the slides range up in terror to culminate in **The Black Hole**, where you corkscrew down in total darkness, carried by a flow that's fed by 4,000 kilograms (almost 5 tons) of water a minute. In between, there's a loop-the-loop tubular slide, the 61-metre (200-foot) Blue Niagara, and many more.

In **Bomb Bay**, riders climb up to a compartment shaped like a large bomb and are then manoeuvered over a six-storey waterslide. Control is entirely in the hands of the ride operator, who may well just let you sweat it out before opening the door and watching you free fall 23 metres (76 feet) into the water below.

Other highlights include the six-storey **Fuji Flyer,** which sends its four-passenger toboggan careening through steep, banked curves, and **The Surge,** a tube ride that will leave you longing for the placid comfort of an air mattress in an old-fashioned swimming pool.

Saying hello to a killer whale at Sea World.

Lifeguards are always on hand to make sure people do not take risks, break the rules, or get into difficulties. Wave machines generate regular 1.2-metre (4-foot) rollers for body-surfing in a big pool. For a more tranquil experience, you can meander along Lazy River on a rubber tube.

It's all a great way to cool off and take a break from the "dry" theme parks. The obvious question is: How does Wet 'n' Wild compare with Disney's Typhoon Lagoon (see page 59)? The answer is, Wet 'n' Wild offers more slides, and some are indeed wilder, so if you're looking for pure thrills, this is the place to be. Typhoon Lagoon, on the other hand, has more beach, more shade, and a bigger wave pool.

Downtown Orlando

In downtown Orlando, old and run-down buildings clustered around a once-shabby railway station have been cleverly restored and extended to create the popular **Church Street Station**, a wonderful cluster of colourful and eclectic shops, food and entertainment outlets, arcaded streets, and a real, shiny steam locomotive. It's all open — though fairly quiet — during the day, but after about 5:00 P.M. the shows start up and you have to pay to go in.

The shows to choose from include a turn-of-the-century-style saloon along with cancan dancers and New Orleans jazz, **Rosie O'Grady's Good Time Emporium**, and a disco, **Phineas Phogg's Balloon Works**. Just across the street is the **Cheyenne Saloon and Opera House**, a three-level extravaganza of wood panelling, brass and stained glass, a top-class country band, an all-singing, all-dancing show, and Western food. Now that more people have come to this part of town, there are also plenty of restaurants, bars, clubs, and discos.

West of Church Street and across the I-4 highway, the **Performing Arts Center** puts on concerts, touring ballet, and opera; the **Arena** is home to a top-flight professional basketball team, the Orlando Magic; and the **Citrus Bowl** is a football stadium seating 70,000.

Not to be missed on the itinerary of sports fans is the spanking new **Walt Disney World International Sports Center,** which houses the Atlanta Braves baseball team for spring training. The 7,500-seat baseball stadium is part of a busy ath-

Bombing away at Wet 'n' Wild's Bomb Bay.

letic complex featuring six basketball courts, training rooms, softball fields, 12 tennis courts, and a golf driving range. This 81-hectare (200-acre) site, with its multimillion-dollar price tag, gives Disney a new realm devoted to sports-related attractions. Watch out for a muscled, baseball-toting Mickey.

Wealthy suburbs start just north of here. At Loch Haven Park (take exit 43 off the I-4 for Princeton Street and go east for 1.6 km/1 mile), the **Orlando Museum of Art** has recently reopened its doors after a 9,500-square-metre (31,000-square-foot) expansion. Now on the radar of nationally touring shows, the museum hosted the blockbuster "Imperial Tombs of China" exhibit in 1997. Loan exhibitions alternate American and African art, but the greatest strength is in the pre-Columbian pieces from Peru and Mexico, dating from 2000 B.C. to A.D. 1500.

Another time frame, B.D. (before Disney), persists in **Winter Park**, a posh district where wealthy northerners came to spend the winter as long ago as 1890. Now the millionaires' mansions are joined by chic restaurants, stylish hotels, and fashionable shops. The **Morse Museum of American Art** (445 Park Avenue) is a magnet for lovers of Art-Nouveau glass, and home to an unrivalled collection of Tiffany lamps, vases, and beautiful windows rescued from the fire which destroyed the home of Louis Tiffany (son of the jewellery maker, Charles).

Inhabiting a brand-new, $44 million facility, the **Orlando Science Center** offers ten exhibit halls showing off the latest in technological wonders, plus planetarium shows in its large-format movie theatre, the **Cine Dome.** One of the most intriguing exhibits places you in the role of a food particle as it travels through the human body.

Kissimmee

Endless ribbons of highway lined on either side by bill-boards, motels, gas (petrol) stations, T-shirt outlets, and other somewhat tacky tourist traps don't hold out much hope on the way to Kissimmee. Is there a real Kissimmee? Where's the old town that existed before all this? Not at **Old Town**, which is a modern pastiche with food outlets and specialist shops, on route US 192 at No. 5770, near the I-4. It's also home of the **Elvis Presley Museum**, which claims to possess the biggest collection of Presley memorabilia outside Graceland.

You'll find traces of original Kissimmee, the little cattle town founded in 1880, along Broadway and Main Street. There's still a livestock auction each Wednesday morning (at 805 East Donegan Avenue), and a great rodeo takes place here twice a year.

Giant alligator jaws herald the entrance to **Gatorland Zoo** (on route 441 near Kissimmee). The serious purpose of this place is farming the 5,000 alligators and crocodiles (animal lovers stay away) that reside here. You can ride round the park on a train and walk above the kind of swamp where alligators like to live: it covered a large part of Florida pre-theme parks and remnants remain in the Everglades. The party piece at Gatorland is feeding time. The alligators' own meat isn't wasted, and you can try out deep-fried "gator snacks ("you've seen the show, now eat the cast").

You can also buy belts, boots, handbags, and wallets made from their skins.

Aviation buffs should not miss the **Flying Tigers Warbird Air Museum** at Kissimmee Airport (North Hoagland Boulevard entrance). Workers here are geniuses at restoring historic aircraft to full flying condition, and the hangar is full of treasures, including a World War II Mustang, a Thunderbolt, and a B-25 Mitchell. Outside, a dozen 1960s jets are waiting their turn for treatment. From the same airport, you can take a flight in the airship painted like Sea World's *Shamu* which you'll have seen circling over the theme parks. Still more thrilling, they also offer flights in old open-cockpit biplanes.

EXCURSIONS FROM ORLANDO

Cypress Gardens

Go west on the I-4 highway towards Tampa, then take the US 27 exit south and follow signs to Winter Haven, then head right at Waverly and go along route 540 for about 8 km/5 miles.

An easy 65 km (40-mile) drive southwest from Orlando, near the old-established resort of Winter Haven, this 90-hectare (223-acre) lakeside park began as a botanic garden in the 1930s, which in fact makes it Orlando's oldest theme park. Now it's more famous for the spectacular **waterski shows** staged several times a day. Some of the world's champion performers do balletic lifts, acrobatic stunts, and circus clown routines and form human pyramids, while microlight aircraft buzz overhead.

The noisy waterski show contrasts with the usual calm of the gorgeously manicured gardens and, a tradition here, the **southern belles** in crinoline dresses and hooped petticoats who stroll in among the flowers and sit twirling their parasols, trying not to look hot. The Kodak **Island in the Sky** is a circular platform on a mechanical arm which raises a new load of passengers 46 metres (153 feet) every few minutes. It's worth being up there during one of the waterski shows. Back on the ground, **Southern Crossroads** is a replica of an old Florida country town from around the year 1900, complete with shops, restaurants, and collections. A bewildering array of butterflies awaits you in the **Wings of Wonder Butterfly Conservatory**, where more than 1,000 of the dazzling creatures flit about this lovely enclosed greenhouse. Representing 50 different species, the butterflies are truly a wonder to behold. Special exhibits include chrysalis chambers, where newly-metamorposed butterflies unfold their wings for the first time.

Electric boats take you on waterways that wind through the gardens' different environments, from strictly formal to tropical jungle, while guides tell you about the 8,000 species of plants as well as the wildlife. In spite of the efforts of the owners (Busch Entertainment Corporation) to add more attractions — for example a model railway and trapeze artists in a circus tent — there's probably not quite enough to keep you here for a whole day. (You can buy a combined ticket at a discount for the three Busch-owned properties: Sea World (see page 69), Busch Gardens (see page 82), and Cypress Gardens.)

Bok Tower Gardens

Continue past the Cypress Gardens exit on US 27 for 8 km (5 miles), exit on route 17A to Alt. US 27, then turn left on Burns Avenue for about 2.5 km (1½ miles).

Florida's highest hill may be only 99 metres (324 feet) above sea level, but it does stand out from the flat landscape near Lake Wales, southwest of Orlando. It became even more of a landmark when Edward Bok, a Dutch-born

New York writer and publisher founded a 52-hectare (128-acre) nature reserve and garden here and topped it with an elegant 62-metre- (205-foot-) high belfry. Built of pink-and-grey marble carved into a blend of Gothic and Art Nouveau, the octagonal **Bok Singing Tower** houses a 57-bell carillon which rings a variety of gentle tunes every half-hour. They are pre-programmed, but at 3:00 P.M. on most days a live carillonist plays a 45-minute recital of hymns, folk tunes and classics.

The oddly ethereal sound doesn't seem to deter the birds from singing, and the tranquil gardens and pleasant, shaded forest walks make an idyllic contrast to the nearby theme park world of concrete, plastic and excess decibels.

Space Coast

From Orlando take the Beeline Expressway east directly to Cape Canaveral.

It's an easy 80-km (50-mile) drive due east to Titusville from Orlando (via a small toll) to the coast, where America's astronauts are launched into space. The **John F. Kennedy Space Center** sent the first mission to land a man on the moon in 1969. Once home of the early NASA launches, today it is the home of the Space Shuttles. To find out when the next take-off is scheduled, check in the newspaper or telephone 1-407-867-4636.

Whether or not a launch is imminent, it's well worth

They make it look so easy to ski at Cypress Gardens.

visiting **Spaceport USA** (the visitor facilities) at the Kennedy Space Center, just off NASA Causeway linking Route A1A with the US Highway 1. The **Rocket Garden** includes several of the earliest research vehicles and also the kind of launchers that put the first Americans into orbit. It's remarkable how small they look now. You can climb aboard the *Explorer,* a full-sized Space Shuttle used as a trainer.

The **Astronauts' Memorial** honours those who have died in accidents during the course of the space programme. In a significant blend of technology and sculpture, it turns with the sun so that the light is reflected to illuminate their names. Multi-media exhibits and shows explain the amazing technology of space travel, and there is a chunk of real moon rock on display.

There's no charge for the basic visit, but you do have to pay to go on the bus tours and to see the IMAX films. Join the queue for tickets as soon as you can, planning what you want to do before you get to the ticket window. The **Red Bus Tour** takes you to the highlights of the moon landing programme, including the gigantic 158-metre (520-foot) **Vehicle Assembly Building** (VAB), or the world's biggest "room." You won't be able to get close if a shuttle is being prepared for launch, and the bus route may vary for operational reasons, but if all is well you will be able to inspect a huge multi-stage Saturn moon rocket, left over when the last missions were cancelled, as well as the lunar launch pad. At **Mission Control**, a roomful of desks and screens, the technology looks quite archaic by more modern standards — perhaps that's why it worked. The **Blue Bus Tour**, probably more suitable for fanatical fans of rocketry than for the average tourist, deals with the history of the unmanned rocket programme.

New to the tour is the **Apollo/Saturn V Center**, an exhibit with videos and photos documenting the most powerful rocket ever launched by the United States. A 3-D IMAX film, *L-5: First City in Space*, explores a futuristic vision of life among the stars.

Two other 40-minute **IMAX films** projected on a giant 5-storey screen are truly thrilling. *The Dream is Alive* (also shown at the Air & Space Museum in Washington, D.C.) is the story of the Space Shuttle, with a lot of footage shot by the astronauts themselves, inside and outside the orbiting craft. **Destiny in Space** alternates at the theater, in which Leonard Nimoy narrates the fascinating conquest of outer space.

Many missions were launched at the Kennedy Space Center.

The first astronauts used to relax, swim, and surf at **Cocoa Beach**, on the strip of island to the south of the Kennedy Space Center. You could take a leaf out of their book and do the same, though the resort is a lot bigger now. The dunes also make an excellent viewpoint for watching shuttles launch into space.

☛ Busch Gardens

Take the I-4 highway west to Tampa and exit at I-75. From the I-75 take exit 54 and follow the signs.

Only a 75-minute drive from Walt Disney World, in a huge 120-hectare (300-acre) park northeast of Tampa, brewing giants Anheuser-Busch have mounted up the attractions as if trying to outdo all their rivals put together. The theme is turn-of-the-century Africa, with more than 3,400 animals to view, as well as authentic **Moroccan-style architecture**. It's wise to collect the map at the entrance, as the layout is confusing.

The main attraction is the 32-hectare (80-acre) open plain of the **Serengeti**, with big-game animals and herds of grazing zebras and antelopes viewed from cable-cars, a monorail, or an old-fashioned train. There's also an extensive petting zoo for smaller children to enjoy, and the park emphasizes its continuing commitment to breeding endangered species.

At **Myombe Reserve: the Great Ape Domain**, you can hear the call of the wild, where lowland gorillas and chimpanzees reside in their natural environment (it's a good idea to take the self-guided tour). Meanwhile, the **World of Birds** show is one of the best in Florida — definitely not to be missed.

When you've had enough of animals, you can get wet whilst **white-water rafting** on River Congo, screaming down the **Tanganyika Tidal Wave**, with a 17-metre (55-foot) drop, or heading down **Stanley Falls**, a log flume ride. Then you can turn your world upside down on the Python, Scorpion, or Kumba — three death-defying **roller coasters**, or take small children to another area with tamer rides.

There are shows all over the place, including an **ice show**, as well as **Questor**, a thrilling simulator ride. After all the excitement, you can visit the on-site **brewery** and sample the beers at Hospitality House (but only if you are 21 or over).

About 1.5 km (1 mile) from Busch Gardens, **Adventure Island** is a waterpark that offers waterfalls, waterslides, waves, and the Aruba Tuba, opened in 1993, a 128-metre (420-foot) tunnels slide. The park closes in winter and is open weekends only during autumn.

WHAT TO DO

SPORTS

Watersports are a year-round pleasure in Florida's delightful climate. Even in winter, the sun will tempt you out on most days, and the swimming pools will be warm. Add plenty of golf courses, tennis courts, fishing spots, and a host of other sporting facilities and you have a marvellous sports resort.

Boating, Canoeing, and Waterskiing

Walt Disney World is a web of waterways connecting lakes large and small, and almost all of its resorts are on a lake or canal, with their own landing places, or fully fledged marinas. Hundreds of pleasure craft of a dozen different sorts can be hired.

For **sailing**, conditions are best at two big lakes (Seven Seas Lagoon and Bay Lake at the Magic Kingdom Resorts). Both single hulls and catamarans are available. The same lo-

You can take to the water in a dozen different ways along the Florida coastline.

cations also have tow boats, drivers, and all the equipment necessary for **waterskiing**.

The canals around Fort Wilderness are good for **canoeing**, and you can take **pedalos** on the lakes. If you prefer a motor to do the work, take a nippy mini-speedboat, a gentler motorized raft or rubber boat.

Outside Walt Disney World, several resort hotels have lakes and watersports opportunities, or try Ski Holidays (on Lake Bryan Drive) with waterskiing and jet skiing; Splash 'n' Ski (Turkey Lake Road) with sailing, boating, and waterskiing; or Airboat Rentals (on Vine Street, Kissimmee) with airboats and canoes for rental.

Fishing

Stocking of Florida's lakes and canals as well as strict environmental policies mean that fish have flourished. Guests at Walt Disney World are usually surprised to find that fishing is allowed from the shores at Fort Wilderness, and in the canals of the Village Resort (but it is, of course, carefully controlled).

In addition, a few people are taken on Bay Lake in organized expeditions every day, starting at 8:00 A.M. as well as at one or two later times. Reservations are required and the cost is quite high, but there will be a good chance of catching sizeable bass. Tackle, bait, and refreshments are provided.

Outside Walt Disney World, Florida is the perfect place for freshwater lakes and rivers: try Lake Tohopekaliga (or Toho) in Kissimmee.

Golf

With the 1992 opening of two new golf courses, Walt Disney World became the biggest golf resort in Florida: they call it the "Magic Linkdom." The five 18-hole championship courses enjoy a high reputation with professionals as well as amateurs, and there is also a 9-hole course intended for families and novices. Fees are relatively high for Florida (reduced if you can start after 3:00 P.M. March through September, or 2:00 P.M. October through February), but facilities are generally "top hole." Except for the 9-hole walking course, you must hire a cart.

The **Magnolia** and **Palm** courses flank the Disney Inn, near the Magic Kingdom, with the 9-hole **Oak Trail** course adjoining the Magnolia. The **Lake Buena Vista** course, a little narrower and shorter, is in the Disney Village, with its own clubhouse.

The newer **Bonnet Creek Golf Club**, in wooded country just north of Dixie Landings Resort, boasts the **Eagle Pines** and **Osprey Ridge** courses. Although each course has its own character, they're all par-72 and play about 6,400 metres (7,000 yards) from the championship tees. Just because some bunkers are shaped like Mickey's ears doesn't make them any easier to escape — Disney courses have long been used on the U.S. pro tour.

You can rent or buy anything you need for a game of golf from the pro shops at each club, and there's even a video-assisted "clinic" at the Magnolia driving range. Lessons with resident professionals can also be arranged.

Outside Walt Disney World, Orlando has plenty of other golf courses. Try the Hyatt Regency Grand Cypress or the Marriott World Center resort hotels as well as several country clubs, such as the Orange Lake Country Club in Kissimmee, and Timacuan Golf and Country Club, Lake Mary.

Swimming

Apart from the **waterparks,** River Country (see page 61) and Typhoon Lagoon (see page 59), every resort and hotel in Walt Disney World has at least one pool. Many are imaginatively themed around ruined pirate forts, beached ships, grottoes, and mountains, with fun slides for the children. If you want to swim serious laps, the sheer numbers of children can be an obstacle except at the big open pools of the Swan, the Dolphin, and the Contemporary Resort.

Then there are the **beaches**. Walt Disney World may be an hour's drive from the sea, but the lakeside resorts have fine, white sandy shores, trees to provide ample shade, sunbeds to lie on — and the lake water is pure and clean.

Lifeguards are on duty (if not, there will be a sign notifying you of their absence). Disney hotels' pools or beaches are open only to guests staying at Disney-owned accommodation, but many other resort hotels have excellent facilities and most budget hotels or motels have some sort of pool.

Outside Walt Disney World, the exciting waterpark **Wet 'n' Wild** (see page 73) makes for an excellent day out, and **Cocoa Beach**, next to Cape Canaveral, has a fine beach with yearly surfing championships. Further south, making up just a part of the 160 km (100 miles) of beaches, you'll find Satellite Beach and Indialantic Beach, which will be less crowded.

Tennis

Over two dozen tennis courts are scattered around the Walt Disney World Resort — at the Grand Floridian and Contemporary Resorts, the Disney Inn and Fort Wilderness; between the Swan and Dolphin and at the Yacht and Beach Clubs; and at the Village Clubhouse. Probably because most of the guests are either focused on the parks or resting from their efforts therein, you will generally have no problem in making a court reservation. All courts are open from 8:00 A.M. to 8:00 P.M.

Florida's Atlantic and Gulf coasts offer endless sandy beaches which are an easy drive from Orlando.

Tennis rackets and balls can be bought or hired, and if you really want to improve your strokes, sign up for lessons and the video-monitored clinic at the Contemporary Resort.

Outside Walt Disney World, the big resort hotels and country clubs all have courts. Try the Orange Lake Country Club in Kissimmee, or the Orlando Tennis Center.

Other Activities

Volleyball has caught on in Florida: you can play at the Walt Disney World beaches, as well as at Typhoon Lagoon (see page 59) and Fort Wilderness, which also has **basketball** courts (or you can watch the Orlando Magic basketball team in the Arena).

Jogging route maps can be bought at Walt Disney World hotels — the most scenic routes are round the lake at Caribbean Beach, at Disney Village, and at Fort Wilderness. You can hire bicycles at Caribbean Beach, at Dixie Landings, Port Orleans, and Fort Wilderness resorts, as well as at the Recreation Center in Disney Village. Note that bicycles are only to be used in the locale where they are rented, and adventurers beware that bicycling on Orlando sidewalks is strictly prohibited.

Health clubs complete with exercise machines, classes, and other facilities are provided at most resorts in and around Orlando. Guests at Disney will find them at the Contemporary Resort, Grand Floridian, Dolphin, Swan, and Yacht and Beach Clubs and Disney Inn. An especially complete regimen may be found at the villas at the Disney Institute Sports and Fitness Center, which houses cardiovascular equipment, steam rooms, and body therapies.

Trail riding on placid horses is offered at Fort Wilderness, or try Poinciana Riding Stables at Kissimmee. Alternatively, you can go walking and bird-spotting along Fort Wilderness' nature trails, and ice-skating is a whiz at Orlando Ice Skating Palace or the Ice Rink International.

SHOPPING

Because so many shops are inside the theme parks, side-by-side with the attractions (and sometimes attractions in themselves), shopping is often just a matter of checking out what is on offer near to the attraction or ride where you are. The shopping opportunities don't end there, however, and there are many more places to spend located outside the parks, where you don't need a ticket to enter and the parking is free.

At **Disney Village Marketplace**, near the Village Resort and next to Pleasure Island, 18 tree-shaded shops are arranged along the waterfront.

Disneyana Collectibles has the biggest collection of Disney merchandise: clothes, toys, games, and countless souvenirs. Nearby, the shops of **Pleasure Island** are open from 10:00 A.M. and you're free to explore them until 7:00 P.M. Some of the odder outlets in Walt Disney World are here, and they're liable to change names and goods at short notice, so any list may soon date. Among the long term survivors look for: **Animation Gallery**, original and repro Disney art, and **Sid Cahuenga's One-of-a-Kind** autographed photos of stars and original movie posters.

Most of the Walt Disney World shops are designed to sell gifts and souvenirs, or more expensive collectibles. If you are just in need of a typical shopping centre close to Walt Disney World and is a good one, go to **Crossroads of Lake Buena Vista**, situated at the end of the road where most of the Village Plaza "official" hotels are located (or leave the I-4 Highway at SR 535 heading north, and turn immediately right). Here you'll find an excellent super-market with a delicatessen counter, a café and pharmacy, a post office, bookstore, bank, dry cleaners, shoe and clothes shops, and plenty of quick-service restaurants.

For some serious clothing shopping, you'll need to take a trip outside of Walt Disney World to one of the monster **shopping malls** in Orlando — concrete and metal agglom-erations of many famous-name stores.

Here are a few of the main ones: Florida Mall is on Sand Lake Road north of International Drive; Fashion Square Mall is close to downtown Orlando on East Colonial Drive; The Exchange at Old Town and Church Street Station on route US 192 has many shops in amongst the restaurants and entertainment facilities (see page 75).

In addition, each suburb has shopping malls. Park Avenue in Winter Park, north of Orlando, has smart and fashionable shop-ping with the likes of Laura Ashley and Crabtree & Evelyn.

Discount and **"factory outlet" malls** could be worth a visit, if you have the time to rummage through "pile-'em-high-sell-'em-cheap" stocks to find what you want. Try Belz Factory Outlet Mall and Quality Outlet Center, both off Inter-national Drive.

ENTERTAINMENT

Of course, Walt Disney World is another word for entertainment (see page 30 for particular parades), but outside the resort most tastes will be catered for somewhere in the vast Orlando-Kissimmee area. Check the fine-arts guide *The Weekly* or the *Orlando Sentinel*, especially at weekends, for full listings of **concerts** — rock, pop or symphony, ballet, opera, and theatre by local or touring groups.

Nightlife in one of the Church Street clubs in Orlando.

If you have the energy to **dance** after a hard day at the theme parks, clubs and discos operate until 2:00 A.M. Zuma Beach (Orange Avenue, Orlando) recreates surf-and-sand disco on four levels at the former Beacham Theatre. Church Street Station offers nightclubs and discos up and down both sides of an old arcaded downtown street. Alternatively, Wolfman Jack's, Old Town, Kissimmee, offers live rock'n'roll, and Sullivan's Entertainment Complex is a country-and-western dance arena.

Dinner Shows

Food and entertainment packages at an inclusive price are all the rage in the Orlando vacation belt, and some of Disney's resorts offer their own versions. You don't have to be staying there to go, either — you simply need a reservation. That may not be easy for the popular **Hoop-Dee-Doo Musical**

Revue at Fort Wilderness Campground, which offers three nightly shows of energetic song, dance, and comedy in Wild West style, as well as food which is big on "country cookin'."

The **Polynesian Luau** at the Polynesian Resort is the kind of show you might expect to see in Hawaii, with South Seas cuisine adapted to American palates. The same entertainers, along with some of the Disney characters, also present **Mickey's Tropical Luau** for children in the late afternoon.

You can eat and be entertained at the EPCOT Center too, in the Marrakesh (Morocco pavilion, see page 48), and also the Biergarten (German pavilion, see page 47).

Outside Walt Disney World, dinner shows will probably be more raucous, fuelled by unlimited beer or wine. Prices are competitive, there's plenty to eat, and the service is efficient. They've had plenty of practice, doing the same thing each night, but the entertainers manage to keep up a high level of enthusiasm.

Among a dozen options are: **Medieval Times** (Highway 192, Kissimmee), a jousting tournament with expert horsemanship; **King Henry's Feast** (International Drive, Orlando), with the much-married monarch in rollicking form; **Sleuths Mystery Dinner Shows** (Republic Drive, Orlando), where a murder plot is even thicker than the stew; and **Arabian Nights** (Kissimmee, W. Irlo Bronson Memorial Highway), starring horses, acrobatic riders, and chariot races.

Pleasure Island

Conscious that they were losing guests in the evenings to outside attractions, the Disney organization decided to create nightlife of its own. **Pleasure Island** is the result: a complex of bars and dance halls, comedy acts, and live bands. The setting is designed like a rundown, ramshackle port which has been given an expensive facelift. Restaurants and night-clubs inhabit the "old" warehouses, and some of the action takes place in the streets.

You can visit the area free of charge during the day, and the restaurants at any time. To gain entry to any of the nightclubs, you need a ticket, which can be bought at the main entrance point (unless you hold a 5-day Super Pass including admission to Pleasure Island).

The clubs open around 7:00 P.M. (although you won't see too much action from the guests at that early hour), and keep going non-stop until 2:00 A.M. It's hard to predict which will be the liveliest, or when. People tend to hop from one to the other, checking them out, then settling somewhere by 10:00 or 11:00 P.M. Upstairs, the **Mannequins Dance Palace**, with its rotating floor and elaborate lighting system, is the smartest disco. **Rock and Roll Beach Club** features live rock bands, and a disco when the musicians are taking a break. Live country music rules at **Neon Armadillo Music Saloon**, and you'll be wrapped up in the 70s at the newest retro venue at Disney, **8trax**.

The **Adventurers' Club** is an oddity. Is it a museum? A bar? A piece of theatre, or an eccentrics' hangout? It seems sometimes that nothing is happening, and you can sit over a drink and study the jokey relics of outlandish "expeditions." But then some strange character may appear and start to regale you with tall stories. Watch out for special effects: some things may not be quite what they seem.

You will probably have to queue to get into the **Comedy Warehouse**. Hopeful potential comedians as well as some established stand-up comics appear in shows on the hour from 7:00 P.M. to 1:00 A.M.

You need to be age 18 or over to get into the nightclubs (it's 21 in the case of Mannequins Dance Palace and Cage), and 21 or over to be served alcohol. Carry your passport (or U.S. driver's licence) as proof.

In Downtown Orlando, the **Church Street Station** entertainment complex also offers plenty of nightlife (see page 75).

Films

If you're looking for some more sedentary entertainment, all the latest movie releases (not only Disney's) are at the 10-screen AMC complex next to Pleasure Island.

Ticket prices are lower for early evening shows. Disney classics as well as new features are also screened occasionally at resort hotels and at Fort Wilderness.

Disney's Boardwalk and Downtown Disney

In an effort to keep up with its visitors' craving for nightlife, Disney has created a number of new entertainment complexes, sporting clubs, restaurants, bars and shops. At Boardwalk opposite the Beach and Yacht club, the dance scene continues at **Atlantic Dance,** where golden oldies share the turntable with the trendiest dance hits. Those who cannot bear to miss the game will find comfort at **ESPN Club,** where more than 70 monitors broadcast up-to-date scores, post-game commentary, and instant replays. This is one dining area where eating in front of the TV is mandatory. **Jellyrolls** finds chortling comedians trading riffs over grand pianos, and **Big River Grille & Brewing Works** debuts as Disney's first brew pub.

Downtown Disney actually comprises three entertainment areas: Pleasure Island, the Village Marketplace, and Disney's west side. As the newest addition, the west side boasts a theatre, an outdoor stage, and the presence of **Cirque du Soleil,** the critically-acclaimed circus show which will offer performances twice a day.

EATING OUT

Florida is a major producer of beef, fish, and shellfish, salad crops and vegetables, and is a world leader in growing citrus fruit. Fierce competition means that you'll usually get good value for money, especially in the type of food America does well: steaks, barbecues, and fried chicken, combined with a buffet or salad bar. See the list of recommended restaurants on pages 136-143.

Parks in the past were accused of dishing up only fast food laced with fat and sugar, but now the choice is more varied. The old faithfuls are still available, but the overall style is healthier, with plenty of salads and fresh fruit, and frozen yogurt as well as ice-cream. Buffets and full-service restaurants in the theme parks and hotels also cater for mainstream tastes and are rarely adventurous, but, especially in Disney territory, the decor is frequently half the fun.

The Magic Kingdom

Take a trip back in time to Mel's Drive-in..

Only a few restaurants in the Magic Kingdom accept advance reservations: Cinderella's Royal Table in Cinderella Castle, Tony's Town Square, and Liberty Tree Tavern. If you're in more of a hurry, the Crystal Palace is a convenient cafeteria near the central Plaza, and Cosmic Ray's Starlight Café is one prominent quick-service operation. You'll find fast-food stalls dotted all over the park.

The EPCOT Center

You wouldn't go to the Magic Kingdom just to eat, but you might to the EPCOT Center (see pages 136-143 for a list of restaurants). Future World has the usual fast-food and snack stalls as well as two full-service restaurants, but the difference at EPCOT is that each of the countries in World Showcase runs at least one restaurant.

You will need reservations for almost all of the full-service restaurants, which can be made at the Earth Station information centre on the touch-sensitive screens. This must be done on the day, and as soon as you can for the popular places. Lunch reservations are easier, and can be made at any of the restaurants themselves as well as at the Earth Station.

Note: Guests in Disney-owned accommodation can telephone in advance for reservations.

Future World

The two full-service restaurants here are the Land pavilion's Garden Grille and the Coral Reef Restaurant in the Living Seas pavilion. Elsewhere in Future World, you'll find standard fare in both West and East CommuniCore buildings and the Odyssey complex next to World of Motion, and snacks at Pure & Simple in Wonders of Life.

World Showcase

Here we'll follow the same clockwise order as on pp.46-49. In **Mexico** the **San Angel Inn**, overlooking the River of Time boat ride, is an offshoot of a famous Mexico City restaurant. It offers more than the usual Mexican fare found in the United States, though the spices are mild by the standards of the original cuisine. The informal **Cantina de San**

Treat yourself to an international delight in one of the eateries at the World Pavilion at the EPCOT Center.

Angel by the lagoon does, however, have the more familiar tacos, tortillas, and beans.

In the **Norway** pavilion, the **Restaurant Akershus** puts on a magnificent colourful buffet, from salted and spiced herring to hot and cold entrées, Norwegian cheeses, and delicious desserts.

China's **Nine Dragons** restaurant offers various regional styles which range from spicy Szechuan to the more familiar (to British diners at least) Cantonese cuisine.

In the **Germany** pavilion, the courtyard **Biergarten** has wursts, dumplings, sauerkraut roasts, and big steins of beer, plus entertainment by yodellers, musicians, and dancers. A second full-service restaurant, **Sommerfest**, offers sandwiches of bratwurst and a ravishing selection of strudels.

L'Originale Alfredo di Roma Ristorante in **Italy** runs the standard gamut from pastas to *gelati*.

Liberty Inn flies the flag for basic **American** burgers, big sandwiches, and old-fashioned apple pie.

In the **Japan Teppanyaki Dining Rooms**, you sit round a
flat grill where a chef stir-fries the food of your choice. The
Tempura Kiku serves light, deep-fried seafood and vegetables and the **Yakitori House** specializes in grills. Meanwhile, the **Matsu No Ma** lounge caters for the growing
numbers of sushi fans.

Morocco's **Marrakesh** restaurant features couscous and
kebabs, roast lamb, and sweet honeyed desserts.

France's choice is between the elegant **Chefs de France**,
comfortable **Bistro de Paris**, and the open-air **Au Petit Café**
(where you don't need to make a reservation, but may have
to wait for a table).

The **United Kingdom** is represented by the traditional-
style **Rose & Crown Dining Room** where you can fill up
with fish and chips, steak and kidney pie, traditional English
trifle, and English cheeses.

Very conveniently for those without reservations, **Le Cellier**, in the **Canada** pavilion, is a cafeteria (sometimes there
is a long queue). Familiar roasts, salmon, and salads are aug-
mented by French-Canadian dishes, Canadian cheeses, and
maple syrup with desserts.

Disney-MGM Studios

Here, the food is all-American — even the Italian and the
chili — served up amid entertainment themes. You can
make reservations for the four full-service restaurants (see
pages 136-143) at their doors: Mama Melrose's, the Sci-Fi
Drive-In Diner, the Hollywood Brown Derby Grill, and the
50s Prime Time Café.

Coming soon is a new restaurant by magician David Cop-
perfield. The **Magic Underground** will have entrances both
inside and outside the park, so admission is not required. Cop-
perfield will occasionally perform disappearing acts.

Hotels

All the Disney hotels provide the dining amenities which guests expect, but menus also emphasize the themes which make each one of them a bit different (see pages 128-135 for our listing).

One or two out-of-the-ordinary establishments are the Palio in the Walt Disney World Swan; Harry's Safari Bar & Grill in the Walt Disney World Dolphin; and the Beach Club's Cape May Café, with its clambake every night.

Elsewhere in Walt Disney World

Although the clubs on **Pleasure Island** don't open until 7:00 P.M., restaurants operate from 11:00 A.M., and snack spots earlier. **Planet Hollywood's** towering 400-seat restaurant numbers Arnold Schwarzenegger, Sylvester Stallone, and Demi Moore among its celebrity owners. American fare with a Cajun twist dominates, if you can see your food in the midst of all the Hollywood kitsch, that is.

At **Disney Village Marketplace**, Cap'n Jack's Oyster Bar is a fine place from which to watch the sunset. It also offers excellent Maryland crab cake, ceviche, crab claw, and other specialities. Chef Mickey's Village Restaurant has fine views of Buena Vista Lagoon and also offers character breakfasts. The "chef" Mickey Mouse makes an appearance each evening. There is also a seafood restaurant on board the re-tired riverboat *Empress Lilly* (named in honour of Walt Disney's wife, Lillian).

Disney Village Marketplace itself offers more choices, including the *House of Blues* restaurant and music hall, and world-famous chef *Wolfgang Puck's Café*. The independent Plaza hotels have their own restaurants, and the **Crossroads at Lake Buena Vista** has another selection of non-Disney food outlets.

INDEX

HANDY TRAVEL TIPS

An A–Z Summary of Practical Information

A

ACCOMMODATION (See also YOUTH HOSTELS on page 127, and the selection of RECOMMENDED HOTELS starting on page 128)

In high season reservations may be hard to come by, especially at Walt Disney World. Book in advance; even a year may not be too far ahead for Christmas and Easter. State taxes are extra (see page 118).

American hotels/motels usually charge by room rather than number of occupants. Most rooms have two double beds, a private bathroom, and colour television. "Efficiencies" are rooms with kitchenette or separate kitchen and dining area, with dishes, pans, and cutlery.

Peak periods in Orlando are: mid-December to early January; February to April (including Easter); and early June to mid-August. At other times, prices are slightly lower in some Disney accommodations, and may be much lower in non-Disney properties.

Some resort hotels offer special rates to guests who take meals on the premises: inquire about package deals, often including breakfast and dinner, when making reservations.

Larger hotels employ a concierge who can arrange tours, call a taxi, or hire a car for you. Visitors on a budget can economize by making their own arrangements.

AIRPORTS

Orlando (McCoy) International Airport (code ORL or MCO) is 15 km (9 miles) south of downtown Orlando and about 40 km (25 miles) from Walt Disney World. Spacious, glittering, and constantly expanding, it has three terminals, with satellite gates reached by "peoplemover" shuttle trains. There are no baggage trolleys, so although carrying distances are short, wheels are desirable. Disney characters make appearances during the day to greet and wave goodbye to travellers.

Ground transport (see also page 126). Taxis and less expensive shuttle minibuses ply between the airport and Walt Disney World locations, International Drive, downtown Orlando, Kissimmee, and Cocoa Beach. Some hotels operate free shuttle services to and from the airport (check with them); if you are on a package tour, airport transfers may be included. There's a public bus to downtown Orlando.

Check-in time. Arrive 45 minutes before domestic flights, and at least 1 hour before international flights (airlines suggest 2 hours). For flight information, telephone your airline.

Other Florida airports. Miami, Tampa, Fort Lauderdale, West Palm Beach, and Key West also have international airports.

Domestic flights. Air travel is by far the quickest and most convenient way of getting around the U.S. Travellers from abroad can buy a Visit USA ticket, which gives substantial discounts and sets no fixed programme. To benefit, you must buy these before you enter the country or within 15 days of arrival.

Fares change constantly, so it would be wise to consult travel agents for the latest information about special deals.

B

BICYCLE RENTAL

Bikes are available for hire at several Disney accommodations including Fort Wilderness and the Caribbean Beach, Dixie Landings, and Port Orleans Resorts. Locks are included.

C

CAMPING

Camping American-style generally involves recreational vehicles (RVs) such as campers, motor homes, or caravans (trailers). If you are camping the American way, Woodalls publishes the most comprehensive guide, which lists and grades both campgrounds and their facilities. (Incidentally, "campsite" in the U.S. means the specific spot where you put your RV or tent.) Camping by the road, or on private land without permission, is both illegal and unsafe.

Disney's Fort Wilderness Resort has sites where you can put up a tent or park your trailer or RV. If you don't have either, "trailer homes" (fairly luxurious, air-conditioned chalets) are available. You will need a reservation.

Disney & Orlando

CAR RENTAL

Competition keeps rates relatively low. Reserving a car before you arrive is often cheaper. Rental companies are found at all Florida's bigger airports, and it's possible to rent a car at one airport and return it to another. Major operators run buses from airports to their offices.

The well-known rental agencies have higher rental rates, but may include insurance costs in the price; smaller agencies may have little or no insurance included in the rates. You are advised to ensure you have CDW (collision damage waiver), or you will be charged for some/all repairs, regardless of whose fault the collision was. Many inclusive holidays and fly-drive packages promise a free car, but you usually have to pay Florida taxes and CDW when you collect it.

To rent a car you must be over 21 (sometimes 25) with a valid driving licence. Some agencies make exceptions for 18-year-old drivers paying by credit card. For tourists from non-English-speaking countries, a translation of the driving licence is recommended, together with the national licence or an International Driving Permit.

It is generally more convenient to pay with a major credit card than with cash. If you have no card, a deposit will be required. Sometimes cash is refused at night and weekends.

CHILDREN

Florida in general and Orlando's theme parks in particular should be a paradise for children. The rides themselves will appeal to them, but also the hotel pools, games, and the crowds of their peers.

In the parks, walking distances are quite long, but pushchairs (strollers) are available for rent. The sun, heat, and humidity can take their toll, especially due to long waits for popular attractions. Small and nervous children could be disturbed by some rides; take advice from the staff. Even the famous Disney characters can seem frightening to the very young. It might be worth warning children that the characters don't speak! Small children may find stressful the following rides in the theme parks: Walt Disney World's Space Mountain, Big Thunder Mountain Railroad, and Alien Encounter; EPCOT Center's Body Wars; Universal Studios' Back to The Future; Disney-MGM's Star Tours and Tower of Terror; and Sea World's Bermuda Triangle.

Restaurants are used to catering to all ages, and many larger hotels provide a **babysitting** service, playgroups, and special entertainment.

CLIMATE

Winter is usually delightful in central Florida, but there are rainy days and cold spells — temperatures can dip to freezing. On the other hand, winter temperatures can reach the 30°C (80°F), so be sure to pack clothing for every eventuality.

Summer ranges from hot to very hot, with high humidity. From June to October it rains most days, though it is rarely troublesome. Hurricanes are rare. On average, Florida is hit one year in seven and only between July and November, so the chances of your experiencing one are minimal. For a weather report, dial (407) 824-4104.

	J	F	M	A	M	J	J	A	S	O	N	D
°C	22	22	25	28	31	32	33	33	32	29	25	23
°F	71	72	78	83	88	90	91	91	89	84	77	73

The above chart shows average maximum daytime temperatures for Orlando (the U.S. still works on the Fahrenheit scale).

CLOTHING

When it starts to get hot or sticky, Floridians turn on the air-conditioners. These can blow with arctic chill, so don't forget to take a wrap with you when shopping, dining out, or riding in air-conditioned vehicles — including buses.

Casual wear is appropriate round the clock — something light, bright, loose, and made of cotton rather than artificial fibres. If you're likely to go swimming often, bring spare swimwear for a rapid change. Other useful items to pack include an umbrella and comfortable walking or sports shoes.

In theme parks and on their transportation, footwear and a shirt or equivalent top cover are required.

COMPLAINTS

If something goes wrong, you'll probably be able to sort it out on the spot with the well-trained, helpful personnel who are typical of the service industries in Florida, and especially in the well-run theme parks. If they can't deal with your problem, ask for someone more senior. Disney accommodations all have a special service telephone number to call in case of difficulties. In the theme parks, the Guest Services desks will assist you.

CRIME

The big theme parks have their own security personnel, so discreet that you are hardly ever aware of them, but they'll be on hand if you need them. Walt Disney World is probably one of the safest environments on earth, but that doesn't mean you shouldn't look after your property. Lockers are available at all theme parks. Most hotels have a safe for valuables. Never leave money, credit cards, cheque books, cameras, etc., in a hotel room — always use the safe.

Outside the theme parks, beware of pickpockets. Carjackings and highway crimes are also quite frequent; be aware. Buying and selling illegal drugs is a serious offence and Florida has a large force of undercover police officers who are battling to keep drugs out. If you are robbed, tell the police, and obtain a copy of the report for your insurance company. Report stolen credit cards and travellers' cheques immediately. (You should have kept a separate copy of the numbers. Ideally, carry a copy of your airline ticket and passport as well.)

CUSTOMS and ENTRY REGULATIONS

British (U.K.) subjects and some other foreign visitors no longer require a visa to enter the U.S., and can instead obtain a visa waiver form from their travel agent or airline. Canadians need only evidence of their nationality. Citizens of the Republic of Ireland, Australia, New Zealand, and South Africa need a visa (but these rules can change, so check with your U.S. embassy or consulate, or travel agent). The application process can be slow, depending on individual circumstances. When you apply, take documents along which show that you intend to return home.

Duty-free allowance. You will be asked to fill out a customs declaration form before you arrive in the U.S. The following chart shows what main duty-free items you may take into the U.S. (if you are over 21) and, when returning home, back into your own country.

Currency restrictions. A non-resident may take in, free of duty and taxes, articles of up to $100 in value for use as gifts. Don't arrive with any plants, seeds, fruits, or other fresh food, as they're banned. The same goes for liqueur chocolates. Arriving and departing passengers should report any money or cheques totalling over $10,000.

Into	Cigarettes	Cigars	Tobacco	Spirits	and	Wine
U.S.A.	200 or	50 or	2*kg*	1*l* or		1*l*
Australia	250 or	250*g* or	250*g*	1*l* or		1*l*
Canada	200 and	50 and	400*g*	1.4*l* or		1.4*l*
Eire	200 or	50 or	250*g*	1*l* and		2*l*
N Zealand	200 or	50 or	250*g*	1.1*l* and		4.5*l*
S Africa	400 and	50 and	250*g*	1*l* and		2*l*
U.K.	200 or	50 or	250*g*	1*l* and		2*l*

D

DISABLED TRAVELLERS

Accessibility and facilities are excellent at the theme parks and other attractions in Orlando. Special parking is available near the entrances to each park, to the hotels, and to other facilities.

Disney publishes the *Disabled Guests Guidebook for Guests with Disabilities*. Ask at City Hall in the Magic Kingdom and at Information/Guest Services desks in other areas.

Wheelchairs are available for rent in limited numbers in several locations: Magic Kingdom, at the Stroller Shop just inside the main entrance; the EPCOT Center, inside the turnstiles to the left; Disney-MGM Studios, just inside the main entrance at Oscar's Super Service. At Sea World and Universal Studios Florida, they may be rented at the entrance. For some attractions and rides, guests may remain in wheelchairs: for others they may have to be able to leave the wheelchair. Regulations are clearly indicated in leaflets and at the appropriate entrance. Some motorized wheelchairs are available for rent, and some buses and launches can accommodate conventional, but not motorized, wheelchairs. Wheelchair access is available at toilets in all the theme parks.

For hearing-impaired guests there is a TDD (Telecommunications Device for the Deaf) at City Hall (Magic Kingdom), at Guest Services at Disney-MGM and EPCOT, and at Universal Studios.

Sight-impaired guests can borrow complimentary cassettes and tape recorders at the same locations. A deposit is required.

DRIVING

On the road. Drive on the right. In Florida, you may turn right after a stop at a red light, provided that there is no cross-traffic, you have given way to pedestrians, and there is no sign to the contrary. Headlights should be used when it is raining enough for window wipers. Seatbelts for all passengers must be worn at all times and you must carry a driving licence.

Lane discipline differs from European norms. American drivers tend to stick to one lane, making no distinction between "fast" or "slow" lanes (except to some extent on the Interstate network). You may therefore be overtaken on either side, so don't change lanes without careful checking.

Don't drink and drive — driving while intoxicated ("DWI") may get you locked up.

Expressways/motorways. On the high-speed divided highways (expressways), driving follows certain rules. Rather than accelerating up the slip road to join the traffic at its own speed, you hesitate at the top and wait for an opening. A speed limit of 90 km/h (55 mph) operates on many highways, except on expressways in rural areas, where the limit is 105 km/h (65 mph). Other speed limits, typically 48 km/h (30 mph) or 70 km/h (45 mph), apply where indicated. If you keep up with the flow of traffic, you'll have no problem, but go any faster and you'll be pulled over; Florida is said to have some of the strictest speeding enforcement in the country.

If you break down on an expressway, pull over on to the right-hand shoulder, tie a handkerchief to the doorhandle or radio aerial, raise the bonnet, and wait in the car for assistance with windows up and doors locked. At night, use the hazard warning lights.

Tolls. Some of the various types of road in Florida (including the turnpike), as well as many causeways and bridges, collect tolls.

Keep a substantial supply of coins when travelling; most toll areas provide a basket into which you drop the correct coinage, so there's no waiting.

Petrol/gas and services. Florida's service stations have both self-service and full-service pumps, fuel at the latter being more expensive. In some areas it is necessary to pre-pay, especially at night. Some pumps are operated by inserting a credit card (major international cards are accepted). Note that some stations close in the evening and on Sunday. In Walt Disney World, petrol (gas) stations can be found near the main entrance to the Magic Kingdom and at the Crossroads shopping centre.

Most rental cars in Florida are equipped with air-conditioners; if your car is running low on petrol (gas) or overheating, turn off the "air-con" — it's a strain on the engine.

Fluid measures

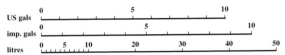

Distance

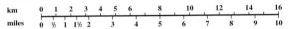

Parking. All the theme parks provide extensive facilities for car parking. There is usually a charge, although at Disney parks it is free if you are staying at Disney-owned accommodation and display the card that you are given when you register. If you do have to pay a parking fee, keep the ticket, since it is valid for all parks used that day. Remember to always make a careful note of the exact spot where you leave your car.

In general, you should park facing in the direction of traffic flow, and nose-in when angle parking is indicated (because Florida cars have no front number plates). Never park next to a fire hydrant, or a kerb painted yellow or red.

Disney & Orlando

Directions. Try to get help planning your route if you don't know the area you are crossing or heading for.

The American Automobile Association offers assistance to members of affiliated organizations abroad. It also provides travel information for the U.S. and can arrange automobile insurance by the month for owner-drivers. Contact the AAA at 1000 AAA Drive, Heathrow, FL 32746-5063; tel. (800) 564-6222.

Road signs. Although the U.S. has started to use the standard international road signs, progress is gradual, and this can lead to some confusion. Detailed below are several common Anglo/American discrepancies:

American	British
Detour	Diversion
Divided highway	Dual carriageway
No passing	No overtaking
Railroad crossing	Level crossing
Traffic circle	Roundabout
Yield	Give way

E

ELECTRIC CURRENT

The U.S. has 110-115 volt 60-cycle AC. Plugs are small, flat, and two-pronged or (more rarely) three-pronged; foreigners will need an adapter for shavers and some other electrical appliances.

EMBASSIES and CONSULATES

Few English-speaking countries maintain a consulate in Florida. The nearest ones to contact are listed below:

Australia: 630 Fifth Avenue, Suite 420, New York, NY 10111; tel. (212) 408-8400.

Canada: 200 South Biscayne Boulevard, Suite 1600, Miami, Florida 33131; tel. (305) 579-1600.

New Zealand: Embassy, 37 Observatory Circle, NW, Washington DC 20008; tel. (202) 328-4800.

Republic of Ireland: 345 Park Avenue, 17th Floor, New York, NY 10022; tel. (212) 319-2555.

South Africa: 333 East 38th Street, 9th Floor, New York, NY 10016; tel. (212) 213-4880.

United Kingdom: 245 Peachtree Street Center Ave., Atlanta, GA 20303; tel. (404) 524-5856; fax (404) 524-3153.

EMERGENCIES (See also MEDICAL CARE on page 117 and POLICE on page 122)

Dial 911, and the operator will ask if you want police, ambulance, or the fire department. All towns and cities have a 24-hour number to call for emergency, if you need a doctor or a dentist.

First-aid posts in Walt Disney World are situated next to the Crystal Palace Restaurant, Main Street, USA (Magic Kingdom); Odyssey Complex, Future World (EPCOT); and the main entrance Guest Services (Disney-MGM Studios). In other areas, you should ask where they are sited.

ETIQUETTE

Foreign visitors will have to get used to American informality. Don't be startled if the hotel desk clerk calls you by your first name. "Thank you" is answered by "you're welcome" or "you're quite welcome," "quite" meaning "very."

G

GETTING TO ORLANDO

Since fares and conditions change frequently, it is advisable to consult travel agents for the latest information.

FROM WITHIN NORTH AMERICA

By air. There are non-stop or direct flights every day to Orlando and other major Florida cities from most large U.S. cities.

By bus. Florida destinations are linked to all major centres by Greyhound, the nation's major bus line, and Trailways. (New York to Orlando by express coach takes around 25 hours.) Smaller bus lines provide a comprehensive local shuttle service between hotels and attractions, and also offer sightseeing tours. Be wary of long-distance, one-day tours: they don't always give sufficient time to visit. Visitors can buy unlimited Ameripasses, valid for a given length of time, to go anywhere in the country by bus at a flat rate.

By rail. Amtrak offers a variety of bargain fares; for example, children may be able to ride free, and there are tour packages with hotel and guide included. It runs a car-carrying train daily between Lorton, near Washington, D.C., and Sanford, near Orlando.

By car. Travellers coming down the East Coast can take the I-95 route via Washington and Savannah. The shortest route from the west coast is the I-10, passing Tucson, El Paso, Houston, and Mobile.

FROM THE U.K.

By air. There are many non-stop and other direct flights from Heathrow and Gatwick to Orlando and Miami. Fares available include first-class, economy, excursion, APEX (Advance Purchase Excursion), business, and special "ticket sales" and promotions available through travel agents. In general, the longer ahead you book, the lower the fare, with the exception of standby fares, which only apply at certain times of year. Some U.S. airlines offer travellers from abroad a discount on the cost of each internal flight, or flat-rate unlimited-travel tickets for specific periods.

Charter flights and package tours. Most charter flights must be booked and paid for well in advance. Many package tours are available: two-centre holidays divide their time between Orlando and one of the beaches (east or west coast of Florida). Other packages on offer combine Orlando with a short cruise, or a spell on a Caribbean island.

Baggage. Allowances for scheduled transatlantic flights are complex, but you are allowed to check in, free, two suitcases of normal size. In addition, one piece of hand baggage which fits easily under the aircraft seat or in the overhead compartment may be carried on board. Confirm size and weight restrictions with your travel agent or air carrier when booking your ticket. It is advisable to insure all luggage for the duration of your trip, preferably as part of a combined travel insurance policy.

FROM ELSEWHERE IN EUROPE

Amsterdam has non-stop flights to Orlando, and many other European cities are linked to Florida by one-stop and other direct flights.

GUIDES and TOURS

Some of the larger attractions provide the services of a guide. In the Magic Kingdom, ask at City Hall (tours begin at 9:15am); in the EPCOT Center inquire at Earth Station. Foreign-language guides are on call to take visitors on a quick tour, including a selection of rides.

LANGUAGE

Most English-speaking foreigners are now familiar with American words and phrases. However, here are a few of the most common Anglo-American linguistic misunderstandings:

U.S.	British
admission	entry fee
bathroom	toilet (private)
bill	banknote (money)
billfold	wallet
check	bill (restaurant)
collect call	reverse charge call
elevator	lift
faucet	tap
first floor	ground floor
gas(oline)	petrol
general delivery	poste restante
liquor	spirits
liquor store	off-licence
pants	trousers
pavement	road surface
purse/pocketbook	handbag
restroom	toilet (public)
second floor	first floor

Disney & Orlando

U.S.	British
sidewalk	pavement
stand in line	queue up
stroller	pushchair
subway	underground
trailer	caravan
underpass	subway
undershirt	vest
vest	waistcoat

LAUNDRY and DRY CLEANING

Coin-operated washing machines and driers are available at all Disney accommodations and many other hotels. You can send laundry through most hotels from Monday to Saturday. Some laundries offer same-day service if garments are dropped off before 9am.

LOST PROPERTY

Each theme park has a Lost Property desk near the entrance. At hotels, ask at the Guest Services desk or telephone Housekeeping.

Air, rail, and bus terminals and many stores have special Lost and Found areas. Restaurants put aside lost articles in the hope that someone will claim them. If your lost property is valuable, contact the police. If you lose your passport, get in touch with your consulate immediately (see page 112).

M

MAPS

The free Guidebook leaflets available at Guest Services/Information desks (City Hall in the Magic Kingdom, Earth Station at EPCOT, and the main entrances of Disney-MGM Studios, Universal Studios, and Sea World) include excellent maps.

Florida Welcome Stations on main highways and ports of entry hand out free maps, and the chamber of commerce or the tourist authority will give you local maps with attractions marked on them.

Service stations dispense maps from vending machines, and car rental agencies give out useful road maps.

MEDICAL CARE (See also EMERGENCIES on page 113)

Foreigners should note that the U.S. does not provide free medical services, and that medical treatment is expensive. Arrangements should therefore be made in advance for temporary health insurance (through a travel agent or insurance company); alternatively, ask at your local Social Security office for information on coverage during your trip.

Clinics offer less prohibitively expensive access to treatment than private practitioners. Emergency rooms of hospitals will treat anyone in need of speedy attention, including hospitalization in a community ward. Disney accommodations offer House Med, an in-room health-care service, but it has to be paid for. House Med also operates a walk-in medical clinic, found at the intersection of I-4 and highway 192.

Beware of the powerful sun. Start with a sunscreen with SPF20 or more, or a complete-block cream at first. Build up your tan gradually in small doses. (Sunscreen products can be bought at many Disney shops.) Drink plenty of water. You can quickly become dehydrated: the warning signs are headaches, lassitude — and grumpy children.

Visitors from the U.K. will find that some medicines sold over the counter at home can only be bought on prescription in the U.S. There's no shortage of drugstores, or pharmacies, and a few of them open late at night. Some pharmacies will deliver to hotels for a fee.

No **vaccinations** are required or recommended for Orlando.

MONEY MATTERS

Currency. The dollar is divided into 100 cents.

Banknotes: $1, $2 (rare), $5, $10, $20, $50, and $100. Larger denominations are not in general circulation. All notes are the same shape and colour (except for the new $100 and $50 bills, which appear slightly different from the other bills).

Coins: 1¢ (called a penny), 5¢ (nickel), 10¢ (dime), 25¢ (quarter), 50¢ (half dollar) and $1. Only the first four are commonly used. You may inadvertently be given Canadian coins in change. They're worth about 15% less than U.S. ones, and they don't work in automatic machines such as telephones.

Disney & Orlando

Banks and currency exchange. Banking hours are usually from 9am to 5pm Monday to Friday, but very few banks change foreign currency. Walt Disney World's banks are a notable exception; their hours are longer and they give a good rate of exchange. You'll find them at City Hall in the Magic Kingdom, at Guest Services windows in all parks, and at the Sun Banks situated in Town Square and across from Disney Village Marketplace. There are also other bank branches opposite Disney Village Marketplace and at the Crossroads of Lake Buena Vista shopping centre. Large hotels are also able to change foreign money. Elsewhere it is simpler as well as safer to travel with travellers' cheques denominated in dollars, major credit cards, or cash in dollars.

When changing money or travellers' cheques, ask for notes with a denomination of $20 or less, which are accepted everywhere, as some establishments will refuse to accept larger notes unless they nearly equal the amount to be paid.

Credit cards. When buying merchandise and tickets, or paying hotel and phone bills, you will invariably be asked "Cash or charge?," meaning you have the choice of paying in cash or by credit card. Businesses are wary of little-known cards, but they'll gladly accept the top American and international cards. You'll sometimes need an additional form of identification when charging your purchase. Some international cards will operate cash dispensers if you know the PIN number, and certain banks will advance cash against the card.

Many service stations will not take money at night, only cards. Outside normal office hours, it's sometimes impossible to rent cars and pay bills with cash.

Travellers' cheques are safer than cash. They can be exchanged quickly, as long as they are in U.S. dollars. Banks will usually want to see your passport or another form of identity document, but many hotels, shops, and restaurants will accept them directly in lieu of cash, especially those issued by American banks. Change small amounts at a time; keep the balance of your cheques in your hotel safe and make a note of serial numbers and where and when you used each cheque.

Prices. Most displayed prices do not include the state sales tax of around 6% — it's added when you pay. The same applies to hotel bills, to which 10 or 11% is added.

The U.S. has a larger spread of prices for the same kind of item than you might find elsewhere, as well as a greater choice. For moderately priced goods, visit the big department and discount stores. Small independent grocery stores, drugstores, and 24-hour convenience stores have price mark-ups of between 10 and 70% over the supermarkets, but independent service stations are cheaper than those of the large oil companies.

PLANNING YOUR BUDGET

To give you an idea of what to expect, here's a list of average prices. They can only be broad guidelines, since inflation continues to push prices upwards.

Airport transfer: Orlando International Airport to Walt Disney World: taxi $42, shuttle $14. Airport to International Drive: taxi $23, shuttle $12.

Babysitters: $5 per hour for one or two children, $1 for each additional child, plus transport expenses. Hotels, including Disney properties charge $9 per hour.

Bicycle rental: $5 per hour, $15 per day, $35-50 per week.

Camping: Fort Wilderness: $35-54 per day, per site (space) with "RV" hook-up. Elsewhere: $15-20.

Car rental: Prices in Florida vary widely. A typical rate for a compact car, unlimited mileage, during high season might be $36 per day, $169 per week, plus insurance.

Entertainment: Cinema $4-8; nightclub/disco $5-20, including cover charge, $4-8 drinks; dinner and show $30-60.

Hotels (double room with bathroom): Walt Disney World: deluxe $240 and up, standard $150, moderate $69. Elsewhere: deluxe $150 and up, moderate $70-100, budget $40-80, motel $30-50.

Laundry: Shirt $1.50, blouse $2.50. Dry cleaning: jacket $5 and up, trousers $3.60, dress $8.25.

Meals and drinks: Continental breakfast $2-10, full breakfast $4-12, lunch in snack bar $5, in restaurant $7-15, dinner $14-40 (more with entertainment), coffee $1.50, beer $2-3, glass of wine $3.50-5.50, carafe of wine $6-10, bottle of wine $9-25, cocktail $4-6.50.

Disney & Orlando

Petrol/gas: $1.15 and up per U.S. gallon (approximately 4 litres).

Taxi (Orlando area): $2.75 for first mile, plus $1.50 per following mile.

Theme parks: One-day ticket (Magic Kingdom *or* Disney-MGM Studios *or* the EPCOT Center *or* the Animal Kingdom): $40.81, child aged 3-9 $32.86. Four-Day Park Hopper $152.64, child $121.90. Five-Day Park Hopper $207.76, child $166.42. Pleasure Island $17.97, Typhoon Lagoon $19.03, Blizzard Beach $19.03, River Country $15.64, Discovery Island $12.67. Universal Studios one-day ticket $40.81, child $32.86. Sea World one-day ticket $39.95, child $32.86.

N

NEWSPAPERS and MAGAZINES

Local newspapers and the national daily *USA Today* are sold in drugstores and from vending machines. Special news-stands carry *The New York Times, The Wall Street Journal,* and *The Miami Herald,* as well as a variety of other newspapers. The *Orlando Sentinel,* one of the better U.S. newspapers, provides information about central Florida and gives TV programmes, opening hours of attractions, pages of grocery store bargains, and coupons for price reductions at various restaurants. Newspapers and magazines from Britain, Germany, France, Italy, etc., are usually available the day following publication in some big supermarkets, shops, and hotels.

O

OPENING HOURS

The three Disney theme parks advertise their opening time as 9am, but that applies to the rides and other attractions. The **Magic Kingdom's Main Street, USA** is open at 8am and the gates at the **EPCOT Center** and **Disney-MGM Studios Theme Park** open at 8:30am. Closing hours vary widely from park to park, day to day and season to season. Check with Disney hotels or Disney information (407) 824-4321 for details.

In the parks, **breakfast and snack places** keep the same hours as the parks: beware that some restaurants may not open until 11am. Elsewhere, breakfast is served from 6 or 7am, lunch from 11am and dinner from as early as 5pm until 10 or 11pm.

Business hours are from 8 or 8:30am to 5 or 5:30pm. **Shops** open from 9 or 10am. Closing hours vary from 5:30 to 9pm (and some supermarkets and convenience stores are open round the clock).

Typhoon Lagoon and River Country: usually opens at 10am and closes at 5pm (later in summer).

Discovery Island: open from 10am to 5pm.

Pleasure Island: clubs and entertainment open at 7pm and close at 2am (the shops are open from 10am).

Universal Studios: open at 9am: closing time varies.

Sea World: open from 9am to 7pm (8:30am to 9pm in summer).

PETS

Pets may *not* be taken into the theme parks, which operate kennels for pets near the entrance to each park. In many places, dogs are not allowed to run free, and they are usually barred from beaches, hotels, restaurants, food shops, and public transport.

PHOTOGRAPHY and VIDEO

Camera shops sell film, but drugstores and supermarkets supply the same — at discount prices. A 2-hour printing service is available in major theme parks and elsewhere. If you are on a short visit, wait until you are home to develop slide film because it may take longer than you think. Don't store film anywhere in the car; it will get so hot in the sun that it may be damaged. Airport security X-ray machines are safe for normal film, whether exposed or unused. Super-fast film may be affected and you should ask for separate inspection.

You can rent cameras and video-cameras for use on Disney property at photographic shops in each park. Video-tape is available for all types of cameras. Note that pre-recorded tapes bought in the U.S.

will not function on European systems (and vice versa); nor will the tapes you make on rented equipment (and conversion is expensive).

POLICE (See also EMERGENCIES on page 113)

City police are concerned with local crime and traffic violations, while Highway Patrol officers (also called State Troopers) ensure highway safety, and are on the lookout for people speeding or driving under the influence of alcohol or drugs. Walt Disney World has its own security force and road patrol. You'll find American police officers to be generally friendly and tolerant of mild transgressions by foreigners.

For emergencies, dial **911** (fire, police, ambulance).

POST OFFICES

The U.S. postal service deals mainly with mail. Telephone and telegraph services are operated by other companies. Post your letters in the blue kerbside boxes. The buff-coloured ones in Main Street, USA are cleared by Disney personnel and the letters taken to a post office. You can buy stamps from City Hall in the Magic Kingdom, and from machines in post office entrance halls after hours (there's also a post office at the Crossroads at Lake Buena Vista shopping centre).

Post office hours are from 8am to 5pm, Monday to Friday, and from 8am to 12 noon on Saturday.

Poste restante (general delivery). You can have mail marked "General Delivery" sent to you care of the main post office of any town. The letters will be held for one month. Take your passport or some other form of ID with you when you go to collect it.

PUBLIC HOLIDAYS

If a holiday, such as Christmas Day, falls on a Sunday, banks and most stores close on the following day.

New Year's Day	1 January
Martin Luther King Jr Day	Third Monday in January
Washington's Birthday *	Third Monday in February

President's Day	February (moveable)
Memorial Day	Last Monday in May
Independence Day	4 July
Labor Day	First Monday in September
Columbus Day *	Second Monday in October
Veterans' Day	11 November
Election Day	November (moveable)
Thanksgiving	Fourth Thursday in November
Christmas Day	25 December

* Shops and businesses open

R

RADIO and TV

Numerous AM and FM radio stations broadcast pop, rock, and country-and-western music, but each city has at least one classical station.

Every hotel room has a television carrying many channels, some 24-hour. Florida news begins around 6pm, national and international news at 6:30 or 7pm, and is broadcast on several networks. Many hotels carry CNN Network, which broadcasts news around the clock.

Commercial American television aims to appeal to the largest possible number, and the amount of advertising tends to annoy those who are not familiar with it. The exceptions are PBS (Public Broadcasting Service) channels, which screen music, drama, and educational programmes, including imports. Special-interest shows and films are aired on cable channels (some are piped free into hotel rooms; some you have to pay for).

RELIGION

There are Catholic services at Disney's Polynesian Resort (Sundays at 8am and 10:15am) and a Protestant service there at 9am. Elsewhere, Saturday newspapers often list the scheduled church services of the following day. Besides Catholic, Episcopalian, Presbyterian, and Methodist churches, you'll see many branches of fundamentalist and Southern Baptist denominations. Jewish services are held at the synagogues in Orlando.

S

SMOKING

Smoking is not permitted on any attraction, ride, or waiting area in theme parks. Most restaurants have designated smoking and non-smoking areas — you will be asked which you prefer. Non-smoking rooms are available at many hotels — ask when you make your reservation or when you check in.

T

TELEPHONES

American telephone companies are efficient and reliable. Phones are found in the streets, at service stations, and in shopping plazas, restaurants, and most public buildings. Directions explaining how to use them are posted on the instrument. To make a local call, lift the receiver, put 25¢ in the slot, wait for the tone, then enter the seven-digit number. The operator will automatically inform you of any additional charge, so have some change ready.

For local directory inquiries enter 411. For local operator assistance, and for help within the same area code, enter 0. For directory assistance in another area, enter 1, then the area code, then 555-1212.

Long-distance calls may be dialled direct from a pay phone if you follow the directions. The prefix 1- is usually needed. If you don't know the correct area code, enter 00 for assistance. Long-distance calls cost more from a pay-phone than from a private one. The international access code is 011, followed by the country code.

Charges are listed in the introduction to the white pages of the telephone directory, with information on person-to-person (personal), collect (reverse-charge) and credit card calls. Some companies no longer accept major credit cards. Numbers with an 800- or 888-

prefix are toll-free, although hotels add a charge when you call out. They may also begin charging after a certain number of "rings" even though there has been no answer, so don't hold on too long.

Fax. You can send faxes from larger hotels and from office service bureaux in some shopping malls.

TIME DIFFERENCES

The U.S. has four time zones; Florida (like New York) is on Eastern Standard Time (EST). Between April and October Daylight Saving Time is adopted and clocks move ahead one hour. The following chart shows the time in other cities in *winter* at noon in Florida:

Los Angeles	**Orlando**	London	Sydney
9am	**noon**	5pm	4am
Sunday	**Sunday**	Sunday	Monday

Dates in the U.S. are often written differently from the European day/month/year system; for example, 1/6/95 means 6 January 1995.

TIPPING

In many restaurants waiters and waitresses earn most of their salary from tips; often they are paid little else. Cinema or theatre ushers and filling-station attendants are not tipped. Some suggestions:

Tour guide	10-15%
Hairdresser/barber	15%
Hotel porter	50¢-$1, per bag (minimum $1)
Taxi driver	15%
Waiter	15–20%

TOILETS/RESTROOMS

Theme parks have many public toilets, marked "restrooms." Elsewhere you can find them in restaurants, railway stations, and large stores. Most are free, but in some places you must deposit a dime or quarter. If there's an attendant, leave a tip.

Disney & Orlando

TOURIST INFORMATION

For information prior to arrival, write to one of the following: Orlando Tourism Bureau, 5 Boyager House, 162-166 Fulham Palace Road, London W6 9ER; tel. (0181) 563-1532; Florida Division of Tourism in Europe, Roebuck House, Palace Street, London SW1 E5BA, tel. (0171) 630-6602; The Walt Disney Company, 3 Queen Caroline Street, London W6 9PE, tel. (0181) 222-2846; Disney World, Box 10,000, Lake Buena Vista, FL 32830-1000, USA; tel. (407) 824-4321.

There can be few places in the world with so much printed tourist literature. Information is dispensed from welcome stations on the main entry routes to Florida, but the chief source of tourist information in any town or resort is the local chamber of commerce office.

In Disney hotels, TV channels 5, 7, and 10 give information, and you can telephone 824-4321 for yet more information.

TRANSPORT (See also AIRPORTS on page 104, CAR RENTAL on page 106, DRIVING on page 110 and GETTING TO ORLANDO on page 113)

The Walt Disney World Resort transportation system is complex, as are the rules about who can use it. They include those staying in Disney accommodation, at the Plaza hotels, or those carrying four- or five-day passes. Additionally, those with Magic Kingdom tickets can use the monorail or ferry to get to its entrance.

Disney buses connect all areas within Walt Disney World. They carry colour codes and prominent signs.

The **Disney World Monorail** links Disney's Magic Kingdom resorts with the Magic Kingdom and the EPCOT Center.

Ferries operate between the TTC and the Magic Kingdom entrance; between the Contemporary Resort and Magic Kingdom, River Country, and Discovery Island; and between the Swan, Dolphin, and Yacht and Beach Club Resorts, Board Walk Inn, and Disney-MGM Studios.

Taxis always carry a roof sign. Most taxis have meters, and the rates are generally painted on the doors. A few taxis wait at theme parks and other attractions towards closing time. Otherwise, you will have to telephone and request a car (consult the *Yellow Pages* under *Taxicabs*).

WEIGHTS and MEASURES (See also Driving on page 110.)

The United States is one of the last countries in the world to change officially from the imperial to the metric system.

Length

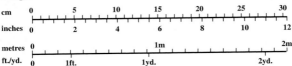

Weight

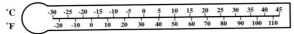

Temperature

YOUTH HOSTELS

The U.S. is not well endowed with youth hostels, although some budget hotels make rooms available to International YHA members at a large discount. There is no age limit. For further information, write to the American Youth Hostels, 733 15th Street, Suite 840, Washington, D.C. 20005.

Recommended Hotels

The Orlando area, including Walt Disney World, has more hotel rooms than anywhere else in the United States. Fierce competition in the highly developed hospitality industry means that you'll be assured of value for money, whether you choose the most luxurious resort, a modest motel, or something between the two.

Here we offer a selection of hotels in each price range, listed in alphabetical order with telephone numbers, and fax numbers where possible. Location may be important, depending on whether you intend to spend most of your time in Disney territory, to visit other attractions, or to travel more widely in central Florida. We have therefore subdivided the list by area, and marked each entry with a symbol indicating the price range, per night, for a double room with bath, excluding breakfast. Taxes of about 10% are added to hotel bills.

In the US, rates are quoted for the room, not per person. If you have more than two occupants, you may be charged a small supplement. Some hotels include a simple Continental breakfast. Always ask about special rate packages, e.g., for stays of a few days.

✪✪✪✪	above $220
✪✪✪	$120-$220
✪✪	$80-$120
✪	below $80

WITHIN WALT DISNEY WORLD

Guests staying in Disney accommodations may use Disney transportation and sports facilities, and have certain privileges when making reservations for shows, dinner, etc. Car parking at the theme parks is free for guests of Disney accommodations, and entry to the parks by Disney transportation is guaranteed, even when they are "full" to others. These advantages, as well as the proximity of accommodations to Disney's theme parks, may compensate for the higher prices of rooms within Walt Disney World.

All-Star Resorts ✪✪✪ *Walt Disney World, Lake Buena Vista, FL 32830; Tel. (407) 939-5000 (sports); Fax (407) 939-7333; Tel. (407) 939-6000 (music); Fax (407) 939-7222.* Sports and music themed resort. Disney's most inexpensive accommodation. 1,920 rooms at each resort.

Board Walk Inn ✪✪✪✪ *Walt Disney World, Lake Buena Vista, FL 32830; Tel. (407) 939-5100; Fax (407) 939-5150.* This most intimate of Disney's deluxe accommodations features New England-style architecture and family-size garden villas. Pool and convention center. 367 rooms, 378 villas.

Caribbean Beach Resort ✪✪ *Walt Disney World, Lake Buena Vista, FL 32830; Tel. (407) 934-3400; Fax (407) 934-3288.* Near the EPCOT Center. Colourful and pretty "village" design around a lake disguises its huge size. Themed pool and marina. 2,112 rooms.

Colorado Springs Resort ✪✪✪ *Walt Disney World, Lake Buena Vista, FL 32830; Tel. (407) 934-6632; Fax (407) 828-5392.* A cluster of buildings evokes a hacienda of the American Southwest. Food court, Mexican restaurant, pools, convention center. 1967 rooms.

Contemporary Resort ✪✪✪✪ *Walt Disney World, Lake Buena Vista, FL 32830; Tel. (407) 824-1000; Fax (407) 824-3539.* A fifteen-storey "vaulting horse" shape, next to Magic Kingdom. Monorail service passes through the huge lobby. Floor show, pools, marina. 1,053 rooms.

Disney Institute ✪✪✪✪ *Walt Disney World, Lake Buena Vista, FL 32830; Tel. (407) 827-4800; Fax (407) 354-2709.* A new neighborhood of villas based around lavish country-style grounds. The Institute offers special education-oriented courses ranging from sports to architecture. Guests learn in the midst of a championship golf course, amphitheatre, and movie theatre. 543 rooms.

Dixie Landings Resort ✪✪ *Walt Disney World, Lake Buena Vista, FL 32830; Tel. (407) 934-6000; Fax (407) 934-5777.* Not far from the EPCOT Center, and very convenient for all areas of Walt Disney World. The Old South theme of plantation homes and wooded setting conceals its enormity. Pools and a waterway and 2,048 rooms.

Grand Floridian Beach Resort ✪✪✪✪ *Walt Disney World, Lake Buena Vista, FL 32830; Tel. (407) 824-3000; Fax (407) 824-3186.* The Grand Floridian offers the marvellous re-creation of Victorian splendour. Monorail service to Magic Kingdom. Pools, marina, beach. 965 rooms.

Polynesian Resort ✪✪✪✪ *Walt Disney World, Lake Buena Vista, FL 32830; Tel. (407) 824-2000; Fax (407) 824-3174.* "South Sea Island" longhouses are set next to the Seven Seas Lagoon. Outside is the monorail service to Magic Kingdom. Pools, beach. 848 rooms, 5 suites.

Port Orleans Resort ✪✪ *Walt Disney World, Lake Buena Vista, FL 32830; Tel. (407) 934-5000; Fax (407) 934-5353.* Not far from the EPCOT Center, and convenient for all areas, this hotel is set in the French quarter of the New Orleans themed area. Themed pool area and waterfront. 1,008 rooms.

Walt Disney World Dolphin ✪✪✪✪ *Operated by Sheraton Hotels, 1500 epcot Resorts Blvd., Lake Buena Vista, FL 32830-2653; Tel. (407) 934-4000; Fax (407) 934-4884.* A short walk to the EPCOT Center's International Gateway. It's a vast tower in salmon and green. Marina, pools. 1,370 rooms, 140 suites.

Walt Disney World Swan ✪✪✪✪ *Operated by Westin Hotels, 1200 Epcot Resorts Blvd., Lake Buena Vista, FL 32830-2786; Tel. (407) 934-3000; Fax (407) 934-4499.* A short walk to the EPCOT Center's International Gateway. Arc-roof tower topped by swans. Marina, pools, beach. 717 rooms.

Walt Disney World Wilderness Lodge ✪✪✪✪ *Walt Disney World, Lake Buena Vista, FL 32830; Tel. (407) 934-7639; Fax (407) 824-3232.* Perched on the shore of Bay Lake, this faux-rustic lodge is styled in a Western motif. Includes pool with boat service to parks. 697 rooms, 31 suites.

Yacht Club & Beach Club Resort ✪✪✪✪ *Walt Disney World, Lake Buena Vista, FL 32830; Tel. (407) 934-7000 (Yacht Club); Fax (407) 934-3450; Tel. (407) 934-8000 (Beach Club); Fax (407) 934-3850.* A short walk to the EPCOT Center's International Gateway. Both based on a 19th-century Massachusetts coast resort. Marina, themed pools, and a beach. 1192 rooms, 41 suites.

DISNEY VILLAGE PLAZA HOTELS

Designated "Official Hotels of Walt Disney World," these are inside Walt Disney World but are not Disney-owned. Entry to the theme parks by Disney bus is guaranteed, and guests may play golf and tennis at Disney Village.

Buena Vista Palace ✪✪✪ *1900 Buena Vista Drive, Lake Buena Vista, FL 32830; Tel. (407) 827-2727; Fax (407) 827-6034.* A lakeside tower complex and convention centre. Tennis, pools, gardens. 1013 rooms.

Courtyard by Marriott ✪✪✪ *1805 Hotel Plaza Boulevard, Lake Buena Vista, FL 32830; Tel. (407) 828-8888; Fax (407) 827-4623.* 14-storey tower and lower annexe. Pools, garden, and family-oriented dining. 321 rooms.

Grosvenor Resort ✪✪✪ *1850 Hotel Plaza Boulevard, Lake Buena Vista, FL 32830; Tel. (407) 828-4444; Fax (407) 828-8192.* Tower block with convention facilities. Tennis, pools. 633 rooms.

Hilton ✪✪✪✪ *1751 Hotel Plaza Boulevard, Lake Buena Vista, FL 32830; Tel. (407) 827-4000; Fax (407) 827-6380.* Huge C-shaped block with a convention centre. Garden, pools, tennis, and restaurants. 787 rooms, 27 suites.

Royal Plaza ✪✪✪ *1905 Hotel Plaza Boulevard, Lake Buena Vista, FL 32830; Tel. (407) 828-2828; Fax (407) 827-6338.* 17-storey block and wings, completely renovated and upgraded. Tennis, pool, garden. 394 rooms.

Travelodge Hotel ✪✪✪ *2000 Hotel Plaza Boulevard, Lake Buena Vista, FL; 32830; Tel. (407) 828-2424; Fax (407) 828-8933.* 18-storey tower. Pool and garden. 325 rooms.

CLOSE TO WALT DISNEY WORLD/KISSIMMEE

Comfort Inn ✪-✪✪ *8442 Palm Parkway, Lake Buena Vista, FL 32830; Tel. (407) 239-7300; Fax (407) 239-7740.* A large budget hotel with the ubiquitous pools. 640 rooms.

Days Inn East of Magic Kingdom ✪✪ *5820 West Irlo Bronson Memorial Hwy. (US 192), Kissimmee, FL 34746; Tel. (407) 396-7969; Fax (407) 396-1789.* Budget hotel. Pools. 604 rooms.

Holiday Inn Maingate East ✪✪ *5678 West Irlo Bronson Memorial Hwy. (US 192), Kissimmee, FL 34746; Tel. (407) 396-4488; Fax (407) 396-1296.* Large family-oriented hotel. Pools and children's entertainment with special "kid suites" for children. 614 rooms.

Howard Johnson's Maingate East ✪ *6051 West Irlo Bronson Memorial Hwy. (US 192), Kissimmee, FL 34746; Tel. (407) 396-4300; Fax (407) 649-8642.* Motel with good-sized rooms, pool. 567 rooms.

Hyatt Regency Grand Cypress Resort ✪✪✪-✪✪✪✪ *1 Grand Cypress Boulevard, Orlando, FL 32836; Tel. (407) 239-1234; Fax (407) 239-3800.* A spacious resort and convention centre with golf courses, tennis courts, pools, a lake, sailing facilities, and equestrian centre. Set in very attractive large gardens. One to four bedroom villas available. 750 rooms.

Larson's Lodge Maingate ✪ *6075 West Irlo Bronson Memorial Hwy. (US 192), Kissimmee, FL 34747; Tel. (407) 396-6100; Fax (407) 396-6965.* Budget hotel but, of course, with pools and water park. 128 rooms.

Marriott Orlando World Center ✪✪✪✪ *8701 World Center Drive, Orlando, FL 32821; Tel. (407) 239-4200; Fax (407) 238-8777.* A towering resort hotel complete with a convention centre, golf course, tennis courts, pools, many restaurants, and splendid large gardens. 1,500 rooms.

Orange Lake Country Club ✪✪ *8505 West Irlo Bronson Memorial Hwy. (US 192), Kissimmee, FL 34746; Tel. (407) 239-0000; Fax (407) 239-1039.* Rooms, apartments, and villas all in a resort complex. Tennis courts, pools, golf course, and watersports on the lake. 1050 rooms/villas.

Radisson Inn Lake Buena Vista ✪✪✪ *8686 Palm Parkway, Lake Buena Vista, FL 32836; Tel. (407) 239-8400; Fax (407) 239-8025.* Large rooms, pools, and gardens. 200 rooms.

Ramada Resort Maingate ✪✪ *2950 Reedy Creek Boulevard, Kissimmee, FL 34747; Tel. (407) 396-4466.* Fine, family-oriented lodgings. Pools, tennis. 278 rooms.

Sheraton Lakeside ✪✪ *7769 West Irlo Bronson Memorial Hwy. (US 192), Kissimmee, FL 34747; Tel. (407) 396-2222; Fax (407) 239-2650.* Lakeside resort, family-oriented. Pools, tennis, large gardens, mini-golf. 651 rooms.

ORLANDO: INTERNATIONAL DRIVE AREA

Caribe Royale Resort Suites ✪✪✪ *14300 International Drive, Orlando, FL 32819; Tel. (407) 238-8000;*

Disney & Orlando

Fax (407) 238-8400. Caters to conferences and families; each room is actually a two-room suite. 1,218 suites.

Country Hearth Inn ✪✪ *9861 International Drive, Orlando, FL 32819; Tel. (407) 352-0008; Fax (407) 352-5449*. Charming hotel with pool. 150 rooms. Every room has its own verandah.

Delta Orlando ✪✪ *5715 Major Boulevard, Orlando, FL 32819; Tel. (407) 351-3340; Fax (407) 351-1429*. A family-oriented budget resort. Pools, garden, tennis, mini-golf. 800 rooms.

Gateway Inn ✪✪ *7050 Kirkman Road, Orlando, FL 32819; Tel. (407) 351-2000; Fax (407) 363-1835*. Family-oriented economy hotel. Pools. 354 rooms.

Holiday Inn ✪✪ *6323 International Drive, Orlando, FL 32819; Tel. (407) 351-4430; Fax (407) 345-0742*. Newly refurbished hotel situated opposite Wet 'n' Wild. 218 rooms.

Peabody Orlando ✪✪✪✪ *9801 International Drive, Orlando, FL 32819; Tel. (407) 352-4000; Fax (407) 351-9177*. A towering 27-storey landmark with a convention centre. Tennis courts and large pool. 891 rooms.

Radisson Twin Towers ✪✪✪ *5780 Major Boulevard, Orlando, FL 32819; Tel. (407) 351-1000; Fax (407) 363-0106*. Hotel set in two glass towers. Convention facilities. Pools, garden. 760 rooms.

Ramada Resort Florida Center ✪✪ *7400 International Drive, Orlando, FL 32819; Tel. (407) 351-4600; Fax (407) 363-0517*. A bright, convenient resort hotel, with indoor and outdoor pools, tennis, and pleasant garden. 396 rooms.

Renaissance Orlando Resort ✪✪✪ *6677 Sea Harbor Drive, Orlando, FL 32821, Tel. (407) 351-5555; Fax (407) 351-9991*. Ten-storey tower and convention complex, but also suited to families. Pools, tennis. 780 rooms.

Sheraton World Resort ✪✪ *10100 International Drive, Orlando, FL 32821; Tel. (407) 352-1100; Fax (407) 352-3679.* Low-rise buildings in large gardens. Pools, mini-golf. 789 rooms.

Universal Towers ✪✪ *5905 International Drive, Orlando, FL; 32819; Tel. (407) 351-2100; Fax (407) 352-2991.* An economical 21-storey round tower hotel with swimming pools and a sauna. 302 rooms.

Westgate Lakes Resort ✪✪✪ *10000 Turkey Lake Road, Orlando, FL 32819; Tel. (407) 352-8051; Fax (407) 345-5384.* Villa complex in large grounds. Tennis courts, pools, golf adjoining. 1,300 rooms.

ORLANDO: NORTH AND DOWNTOWN

Colonial Plaza Inn ✪✪ *2801 East Colonial Drive, Orlando, FL 32803; Tel. (407) 894-2741; Fax (407) 896-9858.* Near Fashion Square. 230 rooms.

Fairfield Inn ✪ *68342 Jamaican Court, Orlando, FL 32819; Tel. (407) 363-1944; Fax (407) 363-1944.* Neat, inexpensive hotel in a complex with restaurants. 134 rooms.

Harley Hotel ✪✪-✪✪✪ *151 East Washington Street, Orlando, FL 32801; Tel. (407) 841-3220; Fax (407) 849-1839.* Downtown lakeside hotel in traditional style. Pool. 264 rooms.

Holiday Inn Orlando North ✪✪ *626 Lee Road, Winter Park, FL 32810; Tel. (407) 645-5600; Fax (407) 740-7912.* Four miles north of downtown Orlando. Pools. 202 rooms.

Orlando Marriott ✪✪✪ *400 West Livingston Street, Orlando, FL 32801; Tel. (407) 843-6664; Fax (407) 648-5414.* Close to downtown. 290 rooms.

Radisson Plaza ✪✪✪ *60 South Ivanhoe Boulevard, Orlando, FL 32804; Tel. (407) 425-4455; Fax (407) 425-7440.* Downtown and close to interstate I-4. Pools, tennis. 337 rooms.

Recommended Restaurants

Everywhere you turn, there's somewhere to eat, and almost everything is open seven days a week. Here we give a selection of full-service restaurants, buffet restaurants, and food courts (multiple outlets sharing a table area); for reasons of space we cannot list even a fraction of the vast number of quick-service restaurants and all-you-can-eat buffets which are well within our lowest price range. Many of the restaurants outside the theme parks serve inexpensive lunch buffets and go over to full service in the evening.

Entries are listed in alphabetical order with a symbol indicating the price range, per person, for a 3-course meal. Drinks, gratuities and 6% sales tax are not included.

✪✪✪	$30 and over
✪✪	$15-$30
✪	up to $15

WITHIN WALT DISNEY WORLD RESORT

Akershus Restaurant ✪✪ *Norway Pavilion, EPCOT (reservations at World Key).* Norwegian buffet of cold and hot dishes, from herring and salmon to goat's cheese and desserts.

Au Petit Café ✪✪ *France Pavilion, EPCOT (no reservations).* Pavement café under canopy with informal French cooking: salads, onion soup, coq au vin, pastries.

Biergarten Restaurant ✪✪ *Germany Pavilion, EPCOT (reservations at World Key).* Veal, smoked pork, *bratwurst,* and other German specialities, with traditional entertainment by musicians, dancers, and yodellers.

Boatwright's ✪✪ *Dixie Landings Resort; Tel. (407) 939-3463.* Like a riverboat under construction. American and Cajun food.

Bonfamilles ✪✪ *Port Orleans Resort, Tel. (407) 939-3463.* In the French Quarter of New Orleans. Creole and American: oysters, crawfish, and salads.

Bongo's ✪✪ *Downtown Disney; Tel. (407) 939-3463*. Cuban cuisine showcasing the tastes of Miami and South Beach.

California Grill ✪✪✪ *Contemporary Resort; Tel. (407) 560-7277*. West Coast cuisine including wood-oven pizzas and pan-seared tuna, with fresh produce flown in daily from California.

Cape May Café ✪✪✪ *Beach Club Resort; Tel. (407) 939-3463*. A New England-style clam bake every night. Seafood buffets.

Cap'n Jack's Oyster Bar ✪✪ *Disney Village Marketplace; Tel. (407) 939-3463*. Crab, lobster, clams, and oysters, plus vegetarian and non-seafood.

Le Cellier ✪✪ *Canada Pavilion, EPCOT (no reservations)*. Cafeteria service of international and Canadian dishes.

Chef Mickey's ✪✪ *Contemporary Resort; Tel. (407) 939-3463*. Family menu of pasta, seafood, and standard American fare. The "chef" Mickey Mouse makes an appearance each evening.

Chefs de France ✪✪✪ *France Pavilion, EPCOT (reservations at World Key)*. Exceptional service and fine, innovative cuisine, including specialities devised by chefs Paul Bocuse and Roger Vergé, as well as master pastry chef Gaston Lenôtre.

Citricos ✪✪✪ *Grand Floridian Beach Resort; Tel. (407) 824-2383*. Florida cuisine with a mediterranean zest.

Colonel's Cotton Mill ✪✪ *Dixie Landings Resort; Tel. (407) 939-3463*. Large food court with Cajun buffet, pizzas and pasta, grills and roasts, fast food, and desserts.

Concourse Steak House ✪✪ *Contemporary Resort; Tel. (407) 939-3463*. American/international menu with prime rib of beef and salad bar. A la carte menu, breakfast and lunch.

Coral Café ✪✪ *Walt Disney World Dolphin Hotel; Tel. (407) 934-4000*. In the Dolphin Hotel (see page 130), à la carte and theme buffet dinners.

Disney & Orlando

Coral Reef Restaurant ✪✪✪ *The Living Seas Pavilion, EPCOT (reservations at World Key).* Dramatically situated restaurant, facing the big artificial reef. The menu concentrates on seafood bisques and grills, seafood, and pasta.

County Fair Restaurant ✪✪ *Hilton at Disney Village/Plaza; Tel. (407) 827-4000, ext. 3091.* Cafeteria and buffet service of American cooking, chiefly barbecued chicken and beef, salads, and desserts.

Dolphin Fountain ✪✪ *Walt Disney World Dolphin Hotel; Tel. (407) 934-4000, ext. 6077.* A 1950s-style "ice-cream parlour" with burgers and fries and other fast-food staples—and ice-cream, of course!

End Zone Food Court ✪✪ *Disney's All-Star Resorts.* Sports-themed arena featuring typical American specialities such as pizza, pastas, sandwiches, and family platters.

50s Prime Time Café ✪✪ *Disney-MGM Studios Theme Park; Tel. (407) 560-7729.* Sit by a 1950s TV playing 1950s sitcoms and eat 1950s favourites such as meatloaf and grilled chicken.

Fireworks Factory ✪✪ *Pleasure Island; Tel. (407) 934-8989.* Interesting variety including barbecues, smoked chicken, citrus chicken. Vegetarian and low-calorie dishes available.

Fulton's Crab House ✪✪✪ *Aboard Empress Lilly riverboat, Disney Village Marketplace; Tel. (407) 934-2628.* New restaurant (opened in 1996). Seafood is the speciality here—shrimp, scallops, and fresh fish.

Garden Grille ✪✪ *The Land Pavilion, EPCOT (reservations at World Key).* Revolving restaurant overlooking the ride at the Land Pavilion. The salads and vegetables you eat here come from the pavilion's greenhouses. Charcoal grills.

Garden Grove ✪✪ *Walt Disney World Swan Hotel; Tel. 934-1618.* Spacious greenhouse setting for buffets, serving American-style cooking. Breakfast with Disney characters.

Harry's Safari Bar and Grill ✪✪ *Walt Disney World Dolphin Hotel; Tel. (407) 934-4000.* Safari decor and fresh grilled seafood and steaks.

Hollywood Brown Derby Grill ✪✪ *Disney-MGM Studios, Tel. (407) 560-7729.* Salads, grills and pasta in 1930s California revisited.

House of Blues ✪✪ *Downtown Disney, Tel. (407) 939-3463.* Live music every night. Specialties include jambalaya and gumbo.

King Stefan's Banquet Hall ✪✪ *Cinderella Castle, Magic Kingdom, Tel. (407) 824-5520.* Medieval setting, but 20th-century American food. Breakfast with Disney characters.

Liberty Tree Tavern ✪✪ *Liberty Square, Magic Kingdom; Tel. (407) 824-6461.* Decorated in the style of an 18th-century inn. Cooking is American with a New England touch; serving oysters, chowders, pasta, and chicken dishes.

L'Originale Alfredo di Roma Ristorante ✪✪ *Italy Pavilion, EPCOT (reservations at World Key).* Ossobuco and pasta including the speciality—fettuccine Alfredo. Strolling musicians entertain the diners.

Mama Melrose's Ristorante Italiano ✪✪ *Disney-MGM Studios; Tel. (407) 560-7729.* Italian-California cuisine—pasta, brick-oven pizza.

Marrakesh ✪✪✪ *Morocco Pavilion, EPCOT (reservations at Earth Station).* Moroccan specialities: couscous, kebabs, tagine, served to the accompaniment of musicians and a belly-dancer.

Mitsukoshi ✪✪✪ *Japanese Pavilion, EPCOT (reservations at World Key).* Sushi, tempura, and stir-fry reign at this complex of three Japanese eateries. The nearby lounge serves martinis made with sake.

Narcoossee's ✪✪✪ *Grand Floridian Beach Resort; Tel. (407) 824-2383.* Lakeside setting for American cuisine in typically large measures: lobsters, steaks, sundaes.

Disney & Orlando

Old Port Royale ✪✪ *Caribbean Beach Resort; Tel. (407) 934-2830.* Food court with six service outlets offering roasts, barbecues, Italian cuisine, and desserts.

The Outback ✪✪✪ *Buena Vista Palace, Disney Village/Plaza; Tel. (407) 827-3430.* Big steaks and big lobsters are the specialities in this Australian-themed restaurant.

Palio ✪✪✪ *Walt Disney World Swan Hotel; Tel. (407) 934-1281.* Northern Italian cooking in an elegant setting. Strolling musicians accompany the meal.

Planet Hollywood ✪✪ *Pleasure Island; Tel. (407) 827-7827.* Dine among movie memorabilia at this super-star chain restaurant. American fare with a Cajun twist.

Portobello Yacht Club ✪✪ *Pleasure Island; Tel. (407) 934-8888.* Northern Italian and seafood specialities.

Rainforest Café ✪✪ *Walt Disney Village Market Place; Tel. (407) 827-8500.* Eat in the midst of volcanos, tropical greenery, and simulated rainstorms. Good American-style grits.

Rose & Crown ✪✪ *U.K. Pavilion, EPCOT (reservations at World Key).* Traditional British fare: roast beef and Yorkshire pudding, fish and chips, trifle, and cheeses.

San Angel Inn ✪✪✪ *Mexico Pavilion, EPCOT (reservations at World Key).* Situated next to the "River of Time" ride. Serves Mexican dishes ranging from the familiar to the unusual.

Sci-Fi Dine-In Theater Restaurant ✪✪ *Disney-MGM Studios; Tel. (407) 560-7729.* Seating is in mock-ups of 1950s convertibles; watch clips from old sci-fi films as you dine. Serves sandwiches and salads.

Seasons Restaurant ✪✪ *Disney Institute; Tel. (407) 827-4451.* Char-grilled catfish and halibut, soups, sandwiches.

Tony's Town Square Restaurant ✪✪ *Town Square, Magic Kingdom; Tel. (407) 824-6793.* Italian standard fare; pasta dishes are a speciality.

Traders ✪✪ *Travelodge Hotel, Disney Village/Plaza; Tel. (407) 828-2424.* Caribbean sugar plantation house setting, island seafood, and steak dishes from around the world.

Trail's End Buffeteria ✪✪ *Pioneer Hall, Fort Wilderness Resort; Tel. (407) 824-2900.* American cafeteria food, pizzas, Italian buffet Saturday nights.

Victoria & Albert's ✪✪✪ *Grand Floridian Beach Resort; Tel. (407) 824-2383.* Elaborate, elegant, and formal setting; American/Continental menu.

Wild Horse Saloon ✪✪ *Downtown Disney, Tel. (407) 939-3463.* Enjoy lunch and light snacks with western-style flair.

Wolfgang Puck's ✪✪ *Downtown Disney; Tel. (407) 939-3463.* West Coast creations featuring Puck's famous pizza.

Yachtsman Steakhouse ✪✪✪ *Yacht Club Resort; Tel. (407) 934-3356.* Steaks cooked over a wood-fired grill; rack of lamb.

ELSEWHERE IN THE ORLANDO AREA

B-line Diner ✪✪ *Peabody Hotel, 9801 International Drive, Orlando; Tel. (407) 352-4000.* Dishes range from snacks to main meals, 24 hours a day, in chrome-and-glass decor, to the sound of a 1950s jukebox.

Bimini Bay ✪ *Sea World, 7001 Sea World Boulevard; Tel. (407) 351-3600.* Casual diner serving snacks and sandwiches as well as seafood dishes.

El Bohio ✪ *5756 Dahlia Drive, Orlando; Tel. (407) 282-1723.* Authentic Cuban café: dishes include beans, rice, shredded beef, and fried plantain.

Bubbalou's Barbeque ✪✪ *1471 Lee Road, Winter Park; Tel. (407) 628-1212.* Southern-style barbecue spot with a casual atmosphere.

Cafe Tu-Tu Tango's ✪-✪✪ *8625 International Drive, Orlando; Tel. (407) 295-222.* Serves tapas, small appetizer dishes. Artists and a card-reader roam the restaurant.

Disney & Orlando

Capriccio ✪✪✪ *Peabody Hotel, 9801 International Drive, Orlando; Tel. (407) 352-4000.* Genuine Italian country cooking with top-quality fresh ingredients.

Cattleman's Steak House ✪ *2948 Vineland Road, Kissimmee; Tel. (407) 851-7130.* Big steaks grilled over charcoal.

Charley's Steak House ✪✪ *6107 South Orange Blossom Trail, Orlando, Tel. (407) 851-8400.* Steak and seafood with salad bar.

Charlie's Lobster House ✪✪ *Mercado Mall, 8445 International Drive, Orlando; Tel. (407) 352-6929.* Everything in shells or scales, any way you like.

Chatham's Place ✪✪✪ *7575 Phillips Boulevard, Orlando; Tel. (407) 345-2992.* Informally elegant dining, French-influenced and innovative cuisine.

Le Coq au Vin ✪✪ *4800 South Orange Avenue, Orlando; Tel. (407) 851-6980.* Informal, genuinely French country cooking, bistro-style.

Dux ✪✪✪ *Peabody Hotel, 9801 International Drive, Orlando;Tel. (407) 352-4000.* Elegant restaurant with innovative cuisine. No duck served, respecting the hotel's resident mascots.

Enzo's ✪ *Marketplace Shopping Center, 7600 Dr. Phillips Blvd., Orlando; Tel. (407) 351-1187.* Popular local pizza joint serves elegant, Italian-style pies.

Hard Rock Café ✪ *Universal Studios Florida, 5800 Kirkman Road, Orlando; Tel. (407) 351-7625.* Burgers and sandwiches, fries and shakes, to the sound of non-stop rock records. Entry from street as well as from studios.

Lili Marlene's ✪✪ *Church Street Station, Orlando; Tel. (407) 422-2434.* Part of the entertainment complex, in an elaborate 1890s revival setting. Standard American menu.

Little Saigon ✪✪ *1106 E. Colonial Drive, Orlando; Tel. (407) 423-3539.* Light, traditional Vietnamese fare in Orlando's busy Asian community.

Macaroni Grill ✪ *5320 West Highway (US 192). Kissimmee; Tel. (407) 396-6155.* Italian cuisine. Specialities include scaloppine di pollo, saltimbocca, and rack of lamb.

Maison et Jardin ✪✪✪ *430 Wymore Road South, Altamonte Springs, Tel. (407) 862-4410.* Elegant old hillside mansion in a garden setting, rather like a country club. Ambitious international menu.

Ming Court ✪✪✪ *9188 International Drive, Orlando; Tel. (407) 351-9988.* Cantonese and other regional Chinese cooking served in an elaborate setting.

Park Plaza Gardens ✪✪✪ *319 South Park Avenue, Winter Park; Tel. (407) 645-2475.* Elegant garden courtyard in which to try inventive international, Caribbean, and French dishes.

Passage to India ✪ *5532 International Drive. Orlando; Tel. (407) 351-3456.* Indian cuisine, including Tandoori and vegetarian dishes, and serving halal meat.

Pebbles ✪✪ *12551 SR 535, at Crossroads, Lake Buena Vista; Tel. (407) 827-1111.* Ideas from all over the U.S.A. (California, Key West) have gone into the menu and the decor.

Ran-Getsu ✪✪ *8400 International Drive, Orlando; Tel. (407) 345-0044.* Elegant setting for fine Japanese food: sushi, sukiyaki, tempura.

Ruth's Chris Steakhouse ✪✪-✪✪✪ *999 Douglas Avenue, Altamonte Springs; Tel. (407) 682-6444.* Serves typical American cuisine, including steaks, lamb chops, and veal.

Shogun ✪✪ *6327 International Drive, Orlando; Tel. (407) 351-4444.* The American version of a Japanese steakhouse. The chefs are part of the show.

Siam Orchid ✪✪ *7575 Republic Drive, Orlando; Tel. (407) 351-0821.* The taste of Thailand—chilli, coriander, lemon grass—adapted to American palates, unless you tell them to give it to you straight.

ABOUT BERLITZ

In 1878 Professor Maximilian Berlitz had a revolutionary idea about making language learning accessible and enjoyable. One hundred and twenty years later these same principles are still successfully at work.

For language instruction, translation and interpretation services, cross-cultural training, study abroad programs, and an array of publishing products and additional services, visit any one of our more than 350 Berlitz Centers in over 40 countries.

Please consult your local telephone directory for the Berlitz Center nearest you or visit our web site at http://www.berlitz.com.